# The Reality of Prayer

# THE REALITY OF PRAYER

### E. M. BOUNDS

New Edition

**BAKER BOOK HOUSE**
Grand Rapids, Michigan 49516

Copyright © 1991 by Baker Books
a division of Baker Book House Company
P.O. Box 6287, Grand Rapids, MI 49516-6287

ISBN: 0-8010-1012-8

Second printing, August 1995

*Printed in the United States of America*

Scripture quotations are taken from the King James Version of the Bible.

# Contents

# Publisher's Preface

FOR almost a century Edward McKendree Bounds's books on prayer have been classic works, stimulating and inspiring Christians to become prayer warriors. A forceful writer and very deep thinker, Bounds spent the last seventeen years of his life reading, writing, and praying. He rose at 4 A.M. daily for many years, and was indefatigable in his study of the Bible.

As breathing is a physical reality to us, so prayer was a reality for Bounds. He took the command, "Pray without ceasing," almost as literally as animate nature takes the law of the reflex nervous system, which controls our breathing.

Because Bounds so diligently practiced what he preached, he was able to capture the essence of prayer, and his works live on to call today's Christians to higher discipleship and an energetic prayer life.

Baker Book House is pleased to present this new edition of *The Reality of Prayer,* which was originally published in 1924. All type has been reset, and archaic words have been modernized, but we have been careful not to dim the intense spirit and clear challenges of this godly man who lived to pray and write about prayer.

# Introduction

EDWARD MCKENDREE BOUNDS was born in northeastern Missouri on August 15, 1835. His father was instrumental in organizing Shelby County, Missouri, and was an original landholder in the county seat, Shelbyville. Bounds attended the Shelbyville one-room school, where he quickly learned to read and write. Because his father served as county clerk, the Bounds home was used for court sessions. This likely motivated Edward to study law, and he passed the bar exam shortly before he turned nineteen. He practiced law until he was twenty-four and then, somewhat suddenly, felt and answered the call to preach. He ardently read Scripture, savored John Wesley's sermons, and began preaching in a small church in the nearby town of Monticello.

During this time the Missouri populace was torn by dissension over slavery and preservation of the Union. Because Bounds was pastor of a congregation in the recently formed Methodist Episcopal Church, South (resulting from the North-South polarity), he was arrested in 1861 by Union troops in Brunswick, Missouri, and charged as a Confederate sympathizer. He was held (with other noncombatants) in a Federal prison in St. Louis for a year and a half. He then was transferred to Memphis and released in a prisoner exchange between the Union and the Confederacy. Shortly afterward he was sworn in as a Confederate chaplain and served concurrently in the Third Missouri Volunteer Infantry Regiment and the Missouri Fifth Infantry (the units had combined after the fighting at Atlanta).

Bounds comforted and prayed with troops under General John Bell Hood just before one of the most severe encounters in the Civil War erupted in the Battle of Franklin (the last great charge mounted by the Confederates). After General Hood's second defeat at Nashville, Bounds was among Confederate prisoners who were released upon the taking of an oath of loyalty to the United States. He returned to the site of the battle to pastor the Franklin Methodist Episcopal Church, South.

Bounds later was assigned to a pastorate in Selma, Alabama. There he met Emma Elizabeth Barnett from Washington, Georgia. In 1874 Bounds was transferred to St. Louis; he and Emma married in 1876. From this union two daughters, Celeste and Corneille, and a son, Edward, were born. Emma died eight years after they were married. About two years after Emma's death, Bounds married her cousin, Harriet Elizabeth Barnett. To them were born three sons (Samuel, Charles, and Osborne) and three daughters (Elizabeth, Mary, and Emmie). Two children died within a year—Edward, at the age of six, and Charles, shortly after his first birthday.

While in St. Louis, Bounds accepted the position of associate editor of the *St. Louis Advocate*, a regional Methodist journal. After nineteen months in this position he moved to Nashville to become the associate editor of the *Christian Advocate*, the official weekly paper for the entire Methodist Episcopal Church, South, denomination.

In 1894 E. M. Bounds concluded his duties in Nashville. He and his family moved to Washington, Georgia, to live in the Barnett House. Here he spent the final nineteen years of his life engaged in intercessory prayer, writing, and itinerant revival ministry. He typically arose at four o'clock every morning to be alone with God in prayer, usually praying until seven o'clock. E. M. Bounds died in 1913 with only two of his books published, *Preacher and Prayer* and *The Resurrection*. Homer W. Hodge, with some help from another friend of Bounds, Claude L. Chilton, assumed the task of bringing to publication nine more books written by E. M. Bounds.

Claude Chilton captured the essence of the books on prayer by Bounds when he said:

> These books are unfailing wells for a
> lifetime of spiritual water-drawing.
> They are hidden treasures,
> wrought in the darkness of dawn
> and the heat of the noon
> on the anvil of experience,
> and beaten into wondrous form
> by the mighty stroke of the divine.
> They are living voices
> whereby he, being dead,
> yet speaketh!

# 1

# Prayer—A Privilege, Princely, Sacred

THE word *prayer* expresses the largest and most comprehensive approach to God. It gives prominence to the element of devotion. It is communion and fellowship with God. It is enjoyment of God. It is access to God. *Supplication* is a more restricted and more intense form of prayer, accompanied by a sense of personal need, limited to the seeking in an urgent manner of a supply for pressing need. Supplication is the very soul of prayer in the way of pleading for some one thing, greatly needed, and the need intensely felt.

*Intercession* is an enlargement in prayer, a going out in broadness and fullness from self to others. Primarily, it does not center in praying for others, but refers to the freeness, boldness, and childlike confidence of the praying. It is the fullness of confiding influence in the soul's approach to God, unlimited and unhesitating in its access and its demands. This influence and confident trust is to be used for others.

Prayer always, and everywhere is an immediate and confiding approach to, and a request of, God the Father. In the prayer universal and perfect, as the pattern of all praying, it is "Our Father, who art in heaven." At the grave of Lazarus, Jesus lifted up his eyes and said, "Father." In his high-priestly prayer, Jesus lifted up his eyes to heaven, and said, "Father." Personal, familiar, and filial was all his praying. Strong, too, and touching and tearful, was his praying. Read these words of Paul:

> Who in the days of his flesh, when he had offered up prayers and supplications, with strong crying and tears unto him that was able to save him from death, and was heard in that he feared (Heb. 5: 7).

So elsewhere (James 1:5) we have "asking" set forth as prayer: "If any of you lack wisdom, let him ask of God, that giveth to all men liberally, and upbraideth not, and it shall be given him."

Asking of God and receiving from the Lord—direct application to God, immediate connection with God—that is prayer.

In 1 John 5:14 and 15 we have this statement about prayer:

> And this is the confidence that we have in him, that if we ask any thing according to his will, he heareth us. And if we know that he hear us, whatsoever we ask, we know that we have the petitions that we desired of him.

In Philippians 4:6 we have these words about prayer:

> Be careful for nothing, but in every thing by prayer and supplication with thanksgiving, let your requests be made known unto God.

What is God's will about prayer? First of all, it is God's will that we pray. "Jesus Christ spake a parable unto them to this end, that men ought always to pray, and not to faint."

Paul writes to young Timothy about the first things which God's people are to do, and first among the first he puts prayer: "I exhort therefore, that, first of all, supplications, prayers, intercessions, and giving of thanks, be made for all men" (1 Tim. 2:1).

In connection with these words Paul declares that the will of God and the redemption and mediation of Jesus Christ for the salvation for all men are all vitally concerned in this matter of prayer. In this his apostolical authority and solicitude of soul conspire with God's will and Christ's intercession to will that "the men pray everywhere."

Note how frequently prayer is brought forward in the New Testament: "Continuing instant in prayer"; "Pray without ceasing"; "Continue in prayer, and watch in the same with thanksgiving"; "Be ye sober and watch unto prayer"; Christ's clarion call was "watch and pray." What are all these and others, if it is not the will of God that men should pray?

Prayer is complementary, made efficient and cooperative with God's will, whose sovereign sway is to run parallel in extent and power with the atonement of Jesus Christ. He, through the eternal Spirit, by the grace of God, "tasted death for every man." We, through the eternal Spirit, by the grace of God, *pray* for every man.

But how do I know that I am praying by the will of God? Every true attempt to pray is in response to the will of God. Bungling it may be and untutored by human teachers, but it is acceptable to God, because it is in obedience to his will. If I will give myself up to the inspiration of the Spirit of God, who commands me to pray, the details and the petitions of that praying will all fall into harmony with the will of him who wills that I should pray.

Prayer is no little thing, no selfish and small matter. It does not concern the petty interests of one person. The littlest prayer broadens out by the will of God till it touches all words, conserves all interests, and enhances man's greatest wealth, and God's greatest good. God is so concerned that men pray that he has promised to answer prayer. He has not promised to do something general if we pray, but he has promised to do the very thing for which we pray.

Prayer, as taught by Jesus in its essential features, enters into all the relations of life. It sanctifies brotherliness. To the Jew, the altar was the symbol and place of prayer. The Jew devoted the altar to the worship of God. Jesus Christ takes the altar of prayer and devotes it to the worship of the brotherhood. How Christ purifies the altar and enlarges it! How he takes it out of the sphere of a mere performance, and makes its virtue to consist, not in the mere act of praying, but in the spirit which actuates us toward men. Our spirit toward folks is of the life of prayer. We must be at peace with men, and, if possible, have them at peace with us, before we can be at peace with God. Reconciliation with men is the forerunner of reconciliation with God. Our spirit and words must embrace men before they can embrace God. Unity with the brotherhood goes before unity with God. "Therefore if thou bring thy gift to the altar, and there rememberest that thy brother hath ought against thee; leave there thy gift before the altar, and go thy way; first be reconciled to thy brother, and then come and offer thy gift" (Matt. 5:23).

Nonpraying is lawlessness, discord, anarchy. Prayer, in the moral government of God, is as strong and far-reaching as the law of gravitation in the material world, and it is as necessary as gravitation to hold things in their proper sphere and in life.

The space occupied by prayer in the Sermon on the Mount reveals its esteem by Christ and the importance it holds in his system. Many important principles are discussed in a verse or two. The Sermon consists of one hundred and eleven verses, and eighteen are about prayer directly, and others indirectly.

Prayer was one of the cardinal principles of piety in every dispensation and to every child of God. It did not pertain to the business of Christ to originate duties, but to recover, to recast, to spiritualize, and to reinforce those duties which are cardinal and original.

With Moses the great features of prayer are prominent. He never beats the air nor fights a sham battle. The most serious and strenuous business of his serious and strenuous life was prayer. He is much at it with the intensest earnestness of his soul. Intimate as he was with God, his intimacy did not abate the necessity of prayer. This intimacy only brought clearer insight into the nature and necessity of prayer, and led him to see the greater obligations to pray, and to discover the larger results of praying. In reviewing one of the crises through which Israel passed, when the very existence of the nation was imperilled, he writes: "I fell down before the Lord forty days and forty nights." Wonderful praying and wonderful results! Moses knew how to do wonderful praying, and God knew how to give wonderful results.

The whole force of Bible statement is to increase our faith in the doctrine that prayer affects God, secures favors from God, which can be secured in no other way, and which will not be bestowed by God if we do not pray. The whole canon of Bible teaching is to illustrate the great truth that God hears and answers prayer. One of the great purposes of God in his book is to impress on us indelibly the great importance, the priceless value, and the absolute necessity of asking God for the things which we need for time and eternity. He urges us by every consideration, and presses and warns us by every interest. He points us to his own Son, turned over to us for our good, as his pledge that prayer will be answered, teaching us that God is our Father, able to do all things for us and to give all things to us, much more than earthly parents are able or willing to do for their children.

Let us thoroughly understand ourselves and understand, also, this great business of prayer. Our one great business is prayer, and we will never do it well unless we fasten it by all binding force. We will never do it well without arranging the best conditions of doing it well. Satan has suffered so much by good praying that all his wily, shrewd, and ensnaring devices will be used to cripple its performances.

We must, by all the fastenings we can find, cable ourselves to prayer. To be loose in time and place is to open the door to Satan. To be exact, prompt, unswerving, and careful in even the little things, is to buttress ourselves against the evil one.

Prayer, by God's very oath, is put in the very stones of God's foundations, as eternal as its companion, "And men shall pray for him continually." This is the eternal condition which advances his cause, and makes it powerfully aggressive. Men are to always pray for it. Its strength, beauty, and aggression lie in their prayers. Its power lies simply in its power to pray. No power is found elsewhere but in its ability to pray. "For my house shall be called the house of prayer for all people." It is based on prayer, and carried on by the same means.

Prayer is a privilege, a sacred, princely privilege. Prayer is a duty, an obligation most binding, and most imperative, which should hold us to it. But prayer is more than a privilege, more than a duty. It is a means, an instrument, a condition. Not to pray is to lose much more than to fail in the exercise and enjoyment of a high, or sweet privilege. Not to pray is to fail along lines far more important than even the violation of an obligation.

Prayer is the appointed condition of getting God's aid. This aid is as manifold and illimitable as God's ability, and as varied and exhaustless is this aid as man's need. Prayer is the avenue through which God supplies man's wants. Prayer is the channel through which all good flows from God to man, and all good from men to men. God is the Christian's father. Asking and giving are in that relation.

Man is the one more immediately concerned in this great work of praying. It ennobles man's reason to employ it in prayer. The office and work of prayer is the divinest engagement of man's reason. Prayer makes man's reason to shine. Intelligence of the highest order approves prayer. He is the wisest man who prays the most and the best. Prayer is the school of wisdom as well as of piety.

Prayer is not a picture to handle, to admire, to look at. It is not beauty, coloring, shape, attitude, imagination, or genius. These things do not pertain to its character or conduct. It is not poetry nor music. Its inspiration and melody come from heaven. Prayer belongs to the spirit, and at times it possesses the spirit and stirs the spirit with high and holy purposes and resolves.

# 2

# Prayer—Fills Man's Poverty with God's Riches

WE have much fine writing and learned talk about the subjective benefits of prayer; how prayer secures its full measure of results, not by affecting God, but by affecting us, by becoming a training school for those who pray. We are taught by such teachers that the province of prayer is not to get, but to train. Prayer thus becomes a mere performance, a drill-sergeant, a school, in which patience, tranquility, and dependence are taught. In this school, denial of prayer is the most valuable teacher. How well all this may look, and how reasonable soever it may seem, there is nothing of it in the Bible. The clear and oft repeated language of the Bible is that prayer is to be answered by God; that God occupies the relation of a father to us, and that as Father he gives to us when we ask the things for which we ask. The best praying, therefore, is the praying that gets an answer.

The possibilities and necessity of prayer are graven in the eternal foundations of the gospel. The relation that is established between the Father and the Son and the decreed covenant between the two, has prayer as the base of its existence, and the conditions of the advance and success of the gospel.

17

Prayer is the condition by which all foes are to be overcome and all the inheritance is to be possessed.

These are axiomatic truths, though they may be very homely ones. But these are the times when Bible axioms need to be stressed, pressed, repeated, and reiterated. The very air is rife with influences, practices, and theories which sap foundations, and the most veritable truths and the most self-evident axioms go down by insidious and invisible attacks.

More than this: the tendency of these times is to an ostentatious parade of doing, which enfeebles the life and dissipates the spirit of praying. There may be kneeling, and there may be standing in prayerful attitude. There may be much bowing of the head, and yet there may be no serious, real praying. Prayer is real work. Praying is vital work. Prayer has in its keeping the very heart of worship. There may be the exhibit, the circumstance, and the pomp of praying, and yet no real praying. There may be much attitude, gesture, and verbiage, but no praying.

Who can approach into God's presence in prayer? Who can come before the great God, maker of all worlds, the God and Father of our Lord Jesus Christ, who holds in his hands all good, and who is all powerful and able to do all things? Man's approach to this great God—what lowliness, what truth, what cleanness of hands, and purity of heart is needed and demanded!

Everywhere in Scripture we are impressed that it is most important and urgent that men pray, that they be skilled in the homiletic didactics of prayer. That is a thing of the heart, not of the schools. It is more of feeling than of words. Praying is the best school in which to learn to pray, prayer the best dictionary to define the art and nature of praying.

We repeat and reiterate. Prayer is not a mere habit, riveted by custom and memory, something which must be gone through with, its value depending upon the decency and perfection of the performance. Prayer is not a duty which must be performed, to ease obligation and to quiet conscience. Prayer is not mere privilege, a sacred indulgence to be taken advantage of, at leisure, at pleasure, at will, and no serious loss attending its omission.

Prayer is a solemn service due to God, an adoration, a worship, an approach to God for some request, the presenting of some desire, the expression of some need to him, who supplies all need, and who satisfies all desires; who, as a Father, finds his greatest pleasure in relieving the wants and granting the desires of his children. Prayer is the child's request, not to the winds nor to the world, but to the Father. Prayer is the outstretched arms of the child for the Father's help. Prayer is the child's cry calling to the Father's ear, the Father's heart, and to the Father's ability, which the Father is to hear, the Father is to feel, and which the Father is to relieve. Prayer is the seeking of God's great and greatest good, which will not come if we do not pray.

Prayer is an ardent and believing cry to God for some specific thing. God's rule is to answer by giving the specific thing asked for. With it may come much of other gifts and graces. Strength, serenity, sweetness, and faith may come as the bearers of the gifts. But even they come because God hears and answers prayer.

We do but follow the plain letter and spirit of the Bible when we affirm that God answers prayer, and answers by giving us the very things we desire, and that the withholding of that which we desire and the giving of something else is not the rule, but rare and exceptional. When his children cry for bread he gives them bread.

Revelation does not deal in philosophical subtleties, nor verbal niceties and hair-splitting distinctions. It unfolds relationships, declares principles, and enforces duties. The heart must define, the experience must realize. Paul came on the stage too late to define prayer. That which had been so well done by patriarchs and prophets needed no return to dictionaries. Christ is himself the illustration and definition of prayer. He prayed as man had never prayed. He put prayer on a higher basis, with grander results and simpler being than it had ever known. He taught Paul how to pray by the revelation of himself, which is the first call to prayer, and the first lesson in praying. Prayer, like love, is too ethereal and too heavenly to be held in the gross arms of chilly definitions. It belongs to heaven, and to the heart, and not to words and ideas only.

Prayer is no petty invention of man, a fancied relief for fancied ills. Prayer is no dreary performance, dead and death-dealing, but is God's enabling act for man, living and life-giving, joy and joy-giving. Prayer is the contact of a living soul with God. In prayer, God stoops to kiss man, to bless man, and to aid man in everything that God can devise or man can need. Prayer fills man's emptiness with God's fullness. It fills man's poverty with God's riches. It puts away man's weakness with God's strength. It banishes man's littleness with God's greatness. Prayer is God's plan to supply man's great and continuous need with God's great and continuous abundance.

What is this prayer to which men are called? It is not a mere form, a child's play. It is serious, difficult work, the manliest, the mightiest work, the divinest work which man can do. Prayer lifts men out of the earthliness and links them with the heavenly. Men are never nearer heaven, nearer God, never more Godlike, never in deeper sympathy and truer partnership with Jesus Christ, than when praying. Love, philanthropy, holy affiances —all of them helpful and tender for men—are born and perfected by prayer.

Prayer is not merely a question of duty, but of salvation. Are men saved who are not men of prayer? Is not the gift, the inclination, the habit of prayer, one of the elements or characteristics of salvation? Can it be possible to be in affinity with Jesus Christ and not be prayerful? Is it possible to have the Holy Spirit and not have the spirit of prayer? Can one have the new birth and not be born to prayer? Is not the life of the Spirit and the life of prayer coordinate and consistent? Can brotherly love be in the heart which is unschooled in prayer?

We have two kinds of prayer named in the New Testament—prayer and supplication. Prayer denotes prayer in general. Supplication is a more intense and more special form of prayer. These two, supplication and prayer, ought to be combined. Then we would have devotion in its widest and sweetest form, and supplication with its most earnest and personal sense of need.

In Paul's prayer directory, found in the sixth chapter of Ephesians, we are taught to be always in prayer, as we are always in the battle. The Holy Spirit is to be sought by intense supplication, and our supplications are to be charged by his vitalizing, illuminating, and ennobling energy. Watchfulness is to fit us for this intense praying and intense fighting. Perseverance is an essential element in successful praying, as in every other realm of conflict. The saints universal are to be helped on to victory by the aid of our prayers. Apostolic courage, ability, and success are to be gained by the prayers of the soldier saints everywhere.

It is only those of deep and true vision who can administer prayer. These "living creatures," in Revelation 4:6, are described as "full of eyes before and behind," "full of eyes within." Eyes are for seeing. Clearness, intensity, and perfection of sight are in it. Vigilance and profound insight are in it, the faculty of knowing. It is by prayer that the eyes of our hearts are opened. Clear, profound knowledge of the mysteries of grace is secured by prayer. These "living creatures" had eyes "within and without." They were "full of eyes." The highest form of life is intelligent. Ignorance is degrading and low, in the spiritual realm as it is in other realms. Prayer gives us eyes to see God. Prayer is seeing God. The prayer life is knowledge without and within. All vigilance without, all vigilance within. There can be no intelligent prayer without knowledge within. Our inner condition and our inner needs must be felt and known.

It takes prayer to minister. It takes life, the highest form of life, to minister. Prayer is the highest intelligence, the profoundest wisdom, the most vital, the most joyous, the most efficacious, the most powerful of all vocations. It is life, radiant, transporting, eternal life. Away with dry forms, with dead, cold habits of prayer! Away with sterile routine, with senseless performances, and petty playthings in prayer! Let us get at the serious work, the chief business of men, that of prayer. Let us work at it skillfully. Let us seek to be adept in this great work of praying. Let us be master-workmen, in this high art of praying. Let us be so in the habit of prayer, so devoted to prayer, so filled with its rich spices, so ardent by its holy flame, that all heaven and earth will be perfumed by its aroma, and nations yet in the womb will be blest by our prayers. Heaven will be fuller and brighter in glorious inhabitants, earth will be better prepared for its bridal day, and hell robbed of many of its victims, because we have lived to pray.

There is not only a sad and ruinous neglect of any attempt to pray, but there is an immense waste in the seeming praying which is done, as official praying, state praying, mere habit praying. Men cleave to the form and semblance of a thing after the heart and reality have gone out of it. This finds illustrations in many who seem to pray. Formal praying has a strong hold and a strong following.

Hannah's statement to Eli and her defense against his charge of hypocrisy was: "I have poured out my soul before the Lord." God's serious promise to the Jews was,

> Then shall ye call upon me, and ye shall go and pray unto me, and I will hearken unto you. And ye shall seek me, and find me, when ye shall search for me with all your heart (Jer. 29:12).

Let all the present day praying be measured by these standards, "Pouring out the soul before God," and "Seeking with all the heart," and how much of it will be found to be mere form, waste, worthless. James says of Elijah that he "prayed with prayer." In Paul's directions to Timothy about prayer (1 Tim. 1:8) we have a comprehensive verbal description of prayer in its different departments, or varied manifestations. They are all in the plural form, supplications, prayers, and intercessions. They declare the many-sidedness, the endless diversity, and the necessity of going beyond the formal simplicity of a single prayer, and press and add prayer upon prayer, supplication to supplication, intercession over and over again, until the combined force of prayers in their most superlative modes, unite their aggregation and pressure with cumulative power to our praying. The unlimited superlative and the unlimited plural are the only measures of prayer. The one term of "prayer" is the common and comprehensive one for the act, the duty, the spirit, and the service we call prayer. It is the condensed statement of worship. The heavenly worship does not have the element of prayer so conspicuous. Prayer is the conspicuous, all-important essence and the all-coloring ingredient of earthly worship, while praise is the preeminent, comprehensive, all-coloring, all-inspiring element of the heavenly worship.

# 3

# Prayer—
# The All-Important Essence
# of Earthly Worship

THE Jewish law and the prophets know something of God as a Father. Occasional and imperfect, yet comforting glimpses they had of the great truth of God's fatherhood, and of our sonship. Christ lays the foundation of prayer deep and strong with this basic principle. The law of prayer, the right to pray, rests on sonship. "Our Father" brings us into the closest relationship to God. Prayer is the child's approach, the child's plea, the child's right. It is the law of prayer that looks up, that lifts up the eye to "Our Father, who art in heaven." Our Father's house is our home in heaven. Heavenly citizenship and heavenly homesickness are in prayer. Prayer is an appeal from the lowness, from the emptiness, from the need of earth, to the highness, the fullness and to the all-sufficiency of heaven. Prayer turns the eye and the heart heavenward with a child's longings, a child's trust and a child's expectancy. To hallow God's name, to speak it with bated breath, to hold it sacredly, this also belongs to prayer.

In this connection it might be said that it is requisite to dictate to children the necessity of prayer for their salvation. But alas! Unhappily it is thought sufficient to tell them there is a heaven and a hell; that they must avoid the latter place and seek to reach the former. Yet they are not taught the easiest way to arrive at salvation. The only way to heaven is by the route of prayer, such prayer of the heart which every one is capable of. It is prayer, not of reasonings which are the fruits of study, or of the exercise of the imagination, which fills the mind with wondering objects, but which fails to settle salvation, but the simple, confidential prayer of the child to his Father in heaven.

Poverty of spirit enters into true praying. "Blessed are the poor in spirit, for theirs is the kingdom of heaven." "The poor" means paupers, beggars, those who live on the bounties of others, who live by begging. Christ's people live by asking. "Prayer is the Christian's vital breath." It is his affluent inheritance, his daily annuity.

In his own example, Christ illustrates the nature and necessity of prayer. Everywhere he declares that he who is on God's mission in this world will pray. He is an illustrious example of the principle that the more devoted the man is to God, the more prayerful will he be. The diviner the man, the more of the Spirit of the Father and of the Son he has, the more prayerful will he be. And, conversely, it is true that the more prayerful he is, the more of the Spirit of the Father and of the Son will he receive.

At the great events and crowning periods of the life of Jesus we find him in prayer—at the beginning of his ministry, at the fords of the Jordan, when the Holy Spirit descended upon him; just prior to the transfiguration, and in the garden of Gethsemane. Well do the words of Peter come in here: "Leaving us an example that ye should follow his steps."

There is an important principle of prayer found in some of the miracles of Christ. It is the progressive nature of the answer to prayer. Not at once does God always give the full answer to prayer, but rather progressively, step by step. Mark (8:22) describes a case which illustrates this important truth, too often overlooked:

And he cometh to Bethsaida; and they bring a blind man unto him, and besought him to touch him. And he took the blind man by the hand, and led him out of the town; and when he had spit on his eyes, and put his hands upon him, he asked him if he saw ought. And he looked up, and said, I see men as trees, walking. After that he put his hands again upon his eyes, and made him look up; and he was restored, and saw every man clearly.

Alone he has to take us at times, aside from the world, where he can have us all to himself, and there speak to and deal with us.

We have three cures for blindness in the life of our Lord, which illustrate the nature of God's working in answering prayer, and show the exhaustless variety and the omnipotence of his working.

In the first case Christ came incidentally on a blind man at Jerusalem, made clay, softened it by spittle, and smeared it on the eyes and then commanded the man to go and wash in the pool of Siloam. The gracious results lay at the end of his action—washing. The failure to go and wash would have been fatal to the cure. No one, not even the blind man, in this instance, requested the cure.

In the second case the parties who bring the blind man back their bringing with earnest prayer for cure; they beseech Christ to simply touch him, as though their faith would relieve the burden of a heavy operation. But he took the man by the hand and led him out of the town and apart from the people. Alone, and in secret, this work was to be done. He spat on his eyes and put his hands on them. The response was not complete, rather it was a dawning of light, a partial recovery. The first gracious communication but gave him a disordered vision, the second stroke perfected the cure. The man's submissive faith in giving himself up to Christ to be led away into privacy and alone, were prominent features of the cure, as also the gradual reception of sight, and the necessity of a second stroke to finish the perfect work.

The third was the case of blind Bartimaeus. It was the urgency of faith declaring itself in clamorous utterances, rebuked by those who were following Christ, but intensified and emboldened by opposition.

The first case comes on Christ unawares; the second was brought with specific intent to him; the last goes after Christ with irresistible urgency, met by the resistance of the multitude and the seeming indifference of Christ. The cure, though, was without the interposition of any agent, no taking by the hand, no gentle or severe touch, no spittle, nor clay, nor washing—a word only and his sight, full-orbed, came instantly. Each one had experienced the same divine power, the same blessed results, but with marked diversity in the expression of their faith and the mode of their cure. Suppose, at their meeting, the first had set up the particulars and process of his cure, the spittle, the clay, the washing in Siloam as the only divine process, as the only genuine credentials of a divine work, how far from the truth, how narrow and misleading such a standard of decision! Not methods, but results, are the tests of the divine work.

Each one could say: "This one thing I know, whereas I was blind I now see." The results were conscious results; that Christ did the work they knew; faith was the instrument, but its exercise different; the method of Christ's working different; the various steps that brought them to the gracious end on their part and on his part at many points strikingly dissimilar.

What are the limitations of prayer? How far do its benefits and possibilities reach? What part of God's dealing with man, and with man's world, is unaffected by prayer? Do the possibilities of prayer cover all temporal and spiritual good? The answers to these questions are of transcendental importance. The answer will gauge the effort and results of our praying. The answer will greatly enhance the value of prayer, or will greatly depress prayer. The answer to these important questions are fully covered by Paul's words on prayer: "Be careful for nothing, but in every thing by prayer and supplication with thanksgiving let your requests be made known unto God" (Phil. 4:6).

# 4

# God Has Everything
# to Do with Prayer

PRAYER is God's business to which men can attend. Prayer is God's necessary business, which men only can do, and that men must do. Men who belong to God are obliged to pray. They are not obliged to grow rich, nor to make money. They are not obliged to have large success in business. These are incidental, occasional, merely nominal, as far as integrity to heaven and loyalty to God are concerned. Material successes are immaterial to God. Men are neither better nor worse with those things or without them. They are not sources of reputation nor elements of character in the heavenly estimates. But to pray, to really pray, is the source of revenue, the basis of reputation, and the element of character in the estimation of God. Men are obliged to pray as they are obliged to be religious. Prayer is loyalty to God. Nonpraying is to reject Christ and to abandon heaven. A life of prayer is the only life which heaven counts.

God is vitally concerned that men should pray. Men are bettered by prayer, and the world is bettered by praying. God does his best work for the world through prayer. God's greatest glory and man's highest good are secured by prayer. Prayer forms the godliest men and makes the godliest world.

29

God's promises lie like giant corpses without life, only for decay and dust unless men appropriate and vitalize these promises by earnest and prevailing prayer.

Promise is like the unsown seed, the germ of life in it, but the soil and culture of prayer are necessary to germinate and culture the seed. Prayer is God's life-giving breath. God's purposes move along the pathway made by prayer to their glorious designs. God's purposes are always moving to their high and beneficial ends, but the movement is along the way marked by unceasing prayer. The breath of prayer in man is from God.

God has everything to do with prayer, as well as everything to do with the one who prays. To him who prays, and as he prays, the hour is sacred because it is God's hour. The occasion is sacred because it is the occasion of the soul's approach to God, and of dealing with God. No hour is more hallowed because it is the occasion of the soul's mightiest approach to God, and of the fullest revelation from God. Men are Godlike and men are blessed, just as the hour of prayer has the most of God in it. Prayer makes and measures the approach of God. He knows not God who knows not how to pray. He has never seen God whose eye has not been couched for God in the closet. God's vision place is the closet. His dwelling place is in secret. "He that dwelleth in the secret place of the most High shall abide under the shadow of the Almighty."

He has never studied God who has not had his intellect broadened, strengthened, clarified, and uplifted by prayer. Almighty God commands prayer, God waits on prayer to order his ways, and God delights in prayer. To God, prayer is what the incense was to the Jewish temple. It impregnates everything, perfumes everything, and sweetens everything.

The possibilities of prayer cover the whole purposes of God through Christ. God conditions all gifts in all dispensations to his Son on prayer: "Ask of me," saith God the Father to the Son, as that Son was moving earthward on the stupendous enterprise for a world's salvation, "and I will give thee the heathen for thy inheritance, and the uttermost parts of the earth for thy possession." Hinging on prayer were all the means and results and successes of that wonderful and divine movement for man's salvation. Broad and profound, mysterious, and wonderful was the scheme.

The answer to prayer is assured not only by the promises of God, but by God's relation to us as a Father.

> But thou, when thou prayest, enter into thy closet, and when thou hast shut thy door, pray to thy Father which is in secret; and thy Father which seeth in secret shall reward thee openly (Matt. 6:6).

Again, we have these words:

> If ye then, being evil, know how to give good gifts unto your children, how much more shall your Father which is in heaven, give good things to them that ask him? (Matt. 7:11).

God encourages us to pray, not only by the certainty of the answer, but by the munificence of the promise, and the bounty of the giver. How princely the promise! "All things whatsoever." And when we add to that "whatsoever" the promise which covers all things and everything, without qualification, exception or limitation, "anything," this is to expand and make minute and specific the promise. The challenge of God to us is "Call unto me, and I will answer thee, and show thee great and mighty things which thou knowest not." This includes, like the answer to Solomon's prayer, that which was specifically prayed for, but embraces vastly more of great value and of great necessity.

Almighty God seems to fear we will hesitate to ask largely, apprehensive that we will strain his ability. He declares that he is "able to do exceeding abundantly above all that we can ask or think." He almost paralyzes us by giving us a *carte blanche,* "Ask of me things to come concerning my sons, and concerning the work of my hands, command ye me." How he charges, commands, and urges us to pray! He goes beyond promise and says: "Behold my Son! I have given him to you." "He that spared not his own Son, but delivered him up for us all, how shall he not with him freely give us all things?"

God gave us all things in prayer by promise because he had given us all things in his Son. Amazing gift—his Son! Prayer is as illimitable as his own blessed Son. There is nothing on earth nor in heaven, for time or eternity, that God's Son did not secure for us. By prayer God gives us the vast and matchless inheritance which is ours by virtue of his Son. God charges us to "come boldly to the throne of grace." God is glorified and Christ is honored by large asking.

That which is true of the promises of God is equally true of the purposes of God. We might say that God does nothing without prayer. His most gracious purposes are conditioned on prayer. His marvelous promises in the thirty-sixth chapter of Ezekiel are subject to this qualification and condition: "Thus saith the Lord GOD: I will yet for this be enquired of by the house of Israel to do it for them."

In the second psalm the purposes of God to his enthroned Christ are decreed on prayer, as has been previously quoted. That decree which promises to him the heathen for his inheritance relies on prayer for its fulfillment: "Ask of me." We see how sadly the decree has failed in its operation, not because of the weakness of God's purpose, but by the weakness of man's praying. It takes God's mighty decree and man's mighty praying to bring to pass these glorious results.

In the seventy-second psalm we have an insight into the mighty potencies of prayer as the force which God moves on the conquest of Christ: "Prayer shall be made for him continually." In this statement Christ's movements are put into the hands of prayer.

When Christ, with a sad and sympathizing heart, looked upon the ripened fields of humanity, and saw the great need of laborers, his purposes were for more laborers, and so He charged them, "Pray ye therefore the Lord of the harvest that he will send forth laborers into his harvest."

In Ephesians, chapter three, Paul reminds those believers of the eternal purposes of God, and how he was bowing his knees to God so that eternal purpose might be accomplished, and also that they "might be filled with all the fulness of God."

We see in Job how God conditioned his purposes for Job's three friends on Job's praying, and God's purposes in regard to Job were brought about by the same means.

In the first part of Revelation, (chapter eight) the relation and necessity of saintly prayers to God's plans and operations in executing the salvation of men is set forth in rich, expressive symbol, wherein the angels have to do with the prayers of the saints.

Prayer gives efficiency and utility to the promises. The mighty ongoing of God's purposes rests on prayer. The representatives of the church in heaven and of all creation before the throne of God "have every one of them golden vials full of odours which are the prayers of saints."

We have said before, and repeat it, that prayer is based not simply on a promise, but on a relationship. The returning penitent sinner prays on a promise. The child of God prays on the relation of a child. What the father has belongs to the child for present and prospective uses. The child asks, the father gives. The relationship is one of asking and answering, of giving and receiving. The child is dependent upon the father, must look to the father, must ask of the father, and must receive of the father.

We know how with earthly parents asking and giving belong to this relation, and how in the very act of asking and giving, the relationship of parent and child is cemented, sweetened, and enriched. The parent finds his wealth of pleasure and satisfaction in giving to an obedient child, and the child finds his wealth in the father's loving and continuous giving.

Prayer affects God more powerfully than his own purposes. God's will, words, and purposes are all subject to review when the mighty potencies of prayer come in. How mighty prayer is with God may be seen as he readily sets aside his own fixed and declared purposes in answer to prayer. The whole plan of salvation had been blocked had Jesus Christ prayed for the twelve legions of angels to carry dismay and ruin to his enemies.

The fasting and prayers of the Ninevites changed God's purposes to destroy that wicked city, after Jonah had gone there and cried unto the people, "Yet forty days and Nineveh shall be destroyed."

Almighty God is concerned in our praying. He wills it, he commands it, he inspires it. Jesus Christ in heaven is ever praying. Prayer is his law and his life. The Holy Spirit teaches us how to pray. He prays for us with "groanings which cannot be uttered." All these show the deep concern of God in prayer. It discloses very clearly how vital it is to his work in this world, and how far-reaching are its possibilities. Prayer forms the very center of the heart and will of God concerning men. "Rejoice evermore, pray without ceasing, and in everything give thanks. For this is the will of God in Christ Jesus concerning you." Prayer is the polestar around which rejoicing and thanksgiving revolve. Prayer is the heart sending its full and happy pulsations up to God through the glad currents of joy and thanksgiving.

By prayer God's name is hallowed. By prayer God's kingdom comes. By prayer is his kingdom established in power and made to move with conquering force swifter than the light. By prayer God's will is done till earth rivals heaven in harmony and beauty. By prayer daily toil is sanctified and enriched, and pardon is secured, and Satan is defeated. Prayer concerns God, and concerns man in every way.

God has nothing too good to give in answer to prayer. There is no vengeance pronounced by God so dire which does not yield to prayer. There is no justice so flaming that is not quenched by prayer.

Take the record and attitude of heaven against Saul of Tarsus. That attitude is changed and that record is erased when the astonishing condition is announced, "Behold he prayeth." The deserter Jonah is alive, and on dry ground, with scarce the taste of the sea or the smell of its weeds about him, as he prays.

Out of the belly of hell cried I, and thou heardest my voice.
The waters compassed me about, even to the soul; the depth

closed me round about, the weeds were wrapped about my head. I went down to the bottoms of the mountains; the earth with her bars was about me for ever; yet hast thou brought up my life from corruption, O LORD my God. When my soul fainted within me I remembered the LORD: and my prayer came in unto thee, into thine holy temple.

And the LORD spake unto the fish, and it vomited out Jonah upon the dry land (Jonah 2:2, 5–7, 10).

Prayer has all the force of God in it. Prayer can get anything which God has. Thus prayer has all of its plea and its claim in the name of Jesus Christ, and there is nothing too good or great for God to give that name.

It must be borne in mind that there is no test surer than this thing of prayer of our being in the family of God. God's children pray. They repose in him for all things. They ask him for all things—for everything. The faith of the child in the father is evinced by the child's asking. It is the answer to prayer which convinces men not only that there is a God, but that he is a God who concerns himself about men, and about the affairs of this world. Answered prayer brings God nigh, and assures men of his being. Answered prayer is the credential of our relation to and our representative of him. Men who do not get answers to prayer from God cannot represent him.

The possibilities of prayer are found in the illimitable promise, the willingness and the power of God to answer prayer, to answer all prayer, to answer every prayer, and to supply fully the illimitable need of man. None are so needy as man, none are so able and anxious to supply every need and any need as God.

Preaching should no more fully declare and fulfill the will of God for the salvation of all men, than should the prayers of God's saints declare the same great truth, as they wrestle in their closet for this sublime end. God's heart is set on the salvation of all men. This concerns God. He has declared this in the death of his Son by an unspeakable voice, and every movement on earth for this end pleases God. And so he declares that our prayers for the salvation of all men are well pleasing in his sight. The sublime and holy inspiration of pleasing God should ever move us to prayer for all men. God eyes the closet, and nothing we can do pleases him better than our large-hearted, ardent praying for all men. It is the embodiment and test of our devotion to God's will and of our sympathetic loyalty to God.

In 1 Timothy 2:13 the apostle Paul does not descend to a low plane, but presses the necessity of prayer by the most forceful facts. Jesus Christ, a man, the God-man, the highest illustration of manhood, is the mediator between God and man. Jesus Christ, this divine man, died for all men. His life is but an intercession for all men. His death is but a prayer for all men. On earth, Jesus Christ knew no higher law, no holier business, no diviner life, than to plead for men. In heaven he knows no more royal estate, no higher theme, than to intercede for men. On earth he lived and prayed and died for men. His life, his death, and his exaltation in heaven all plead for men.

Is there any work, higher work for the disciple to do than his Lord did? Is there any loftier employment, more honorable, more divine, than to pray for men? To take their woes, their sins, and their perils before God; to be one with Christ? To break the slavery which binds them, the hell which holds them and lift them to immortality and eternal life?

# 5

# Jesus Christ,
# the Divine Teacher of Prayer

JESUS Christ was the divine teacher of prayer. Its power and nature had been illustrated by many a saint and prophet in olden times, but modern sainthood and modern teachers of prayer had lost their inspiration and life. Religiously dead teachers and superficial ecclesiastics had forgotten what it was to pray. They did much of saying prayers, on state occasions, in public, with much ostentation and parade, but pray they did not. To them it was almost a lost practice. In the multiplicity of saying prayers they had lost the art of praying.

The history of the disciples during the earthly life of our Lord was not marked with much devotion. They were much enamored by their personal association with Christ. They were charmed by his words, excited by his miracles, and were entertained and concerned by the hopes which a selfish interest aroused in his person and mission. Taken up with the superficial and worldly views of his character, they neglected and overlooked the deeper and weightier things which belonged to him and his mission. The neglect of the most obliging and ordinary duties by them was a noticeable feature in their conduct. So evident and singular was their conduct in this regard, that it

became a matter of grave inquiry on one occasion and severe
chiding on another.

> And they said unto him, Why do the disciples of John fast
> often, and make prayers, and likewise the disciples of the
> Pharisees; but thine eat and drink? And he said unto them, Can
> ye make the children of the bridechamber fast, while the bride-
> groom is with them? But the days will come, when the bride-
> groom shall be taken away from them, and then shall they fast
> in those days (Luke 5:33–35).

In the example and the teaching of Jesus Christ, prayer
assumes its normal relation to God's person, God's movements,
and God's Son. Jesus Christ was essentially the teacher of
prayer by precept and example. We have glimpses of his praying which, like indices, tell how full of prayer the pages, chapters, and volumes of his life were. The epitome which covers
not one segment only, but the whole circle of his life, and character, is preeminently that of prayer! "In the days of his flesh,"
the divine record reads, "when he had offered up prayers and
supplications, with strong crying and tears." The suppliant of
all suppliants he was, the intercessor of all intercessors. In
lowliest form he approached God, and with strongest pleas he
prayed and supplicated.

Jesus Christ teaches the importance of prayer by his urgency
to his disciples to pray. But he shows us more than that. He
shows how far prayer enters into the purposes of God. We
must ever keep in mind that the relation of Jesus Christ to God
is the relation of asking and giving, the Son ever asking, the
Father ever giving. We must never forget that God has put the
conquering, inheriting, and expanding forces of Christ's cause
in prayer.

> Ask of me, and I shall give thee the heathen for thine inheri-
> tance, and the uttermost parts of the earth for thy possession
> (Ps. 2:8).

This was the clause embodying the royal proclamation and
the universal condition when the Son was enthroned as the

world's mediator, and when he was sent on his mission of receiving grace and power. We very naturally learn from this how Jesus would stress praying as the one sole condition of his receiving his possession and inheritance.

Necessarily in this study on prayer, lines of thought will cross each other, and the same Scripture passage or incident will be mentioned more than once, simply because a passage may teach one or more truths. This is the case when we speak of the vast comprehensiveness of prayer. How all-inclusive Jesus Christ makes prayer! It has no limitations in extent or things! The promises to prayer are Godlike in their magnificence, wideness, and universality. In their nature these promises have to do with God—with him in their inspiration, creation, and results. Who but God could say, "All things whatsoever ye ask in prayer, believing, ye shall receive?" Who can command and direct "All things whatsoever" but God? Neither man nor chance nor the law of results are so far lifted above change, limitations, or condition, nor have in them mighty forces which can direct and result all things, as to promise the bestowment and direction of all things.

Whole sections, parables, and incidents were used by Christ to enforce the necessity and importance of prayer. His miracles are but parables of prayer. In nearly all of them prayer figures distinctly, and some features of it are illustrated. The Syrophenician woman is a preeminent illustration of the ability and the success of importunity in prayer. The case of blind Bartimaeus has points of suggestion along the same line. Jairus and the centurion illustrate and impress phases of prayer. The parable of the Pharisee and the publican inforces humility in prayer, declares the wondrous results of praying, and shows the vanity and worthlessness of wrong praying. The failure to enforce church discipline and the readiness of violating the brotherhood, are all used to make an exhibit of far-reaching results of agreed praying, a record of which we have in Matthew 18:19.

It is of prayer in concert that Christ is speaking: two agreed ones, two whose hearts have been keyed into perfect symphony by the Holy Spirit. Anything that they shall ask, it shall be done. Christ had been speaking of discipline in the church, how things were to be kept in unity, and how the fellowship of the brethren was to be maintained, by the restoration of the offender or by his exclusion. Members who had been true to the brotherhood of Christ, and who were laboring to preserve that brotherhood unbroken, would be the agreed ones to make appeals to God in united prayer.

In the Sermon on the Mount, Christ lays down constitutional principles. Types and shadows are retired, and the law of spiritual life is declared. In this foundation law of the Christian system prayer assumes a conspicuous, if not a paramount, position. It is not only wide, all-commanding, and comprehensive in its own sphere of action and relief, but it is ancillary to all duties. Even the one demanding kindly and discriminating judgment toward others, and also the royal injunction, the golden rule of action, these owe their being to prayer.

Christ puts prayer among the statutory promises. He does not leave it to natural law. The law of need, demand, and supply, of helplessness, of natural instincts, or the law of sweet, high, attractive privilege—these howsoever strong as motives of action, are not the basis of praying. Christ puts it as spiritual law. Men must pray. Not to pray is not simply a privation, an omission, but a positive violation of law, of spiritual life, a crime, bringing disorder and ruin. Prayer is law worldwide and eternity-reaching.

In the Sermon on the Mount many important utterances are dismissed with a line or a verse, while the subject of prayer occupies a large space. To it Christ returns again and again. He bases the possibilities and necessities of prayer on the relation of father and child, the child crying for bread, and the father giving that for which the child asks. Prayer and its answer are in the relation of a father to his child. The teaching of Jesus Christ on the nature and necessity of prayer as recorded in his life, is remarkable. He sends men to their closets. Prayer must be a holy exercise, untainted by vanity or pride. It must be in secret. The disciple must live in secret. God lives there, is sought there and is found there. The command of Christ as to prayer is that pride and publicity should be shunned. Prayer is to be in private.

> But thou, when thou prayest, enter into thy closet, and when thou hast shut thy door, pray to thy Father which is in secret; and thy Father which seeth in secret shall reward thee openly (Matt. 6:6).

The Beatitudes are not only to enrich and adorn, but they are also the material out of which spiritual character is built. The very first one of these fixes prayer in the very foundation of spiritual character, not simply to adorn, but to compose. "Blessed are the poor in spirit." The word *poor* means a pauper, one who lives by begging. The real Christian lives on the bounties of another, whose bounties he gets by asking. Prayer then becomes the basis of Christian character, the Christian's business, his life, and his living. This is Christ's law of prayer, putting it into the very being of the Christian. It is his first step, and his first breath, which is to color and to form all his afterlife. Blessed are the poor ones, for they only can pray.

> Prayer is the Christian's vital breath,
> The Christian's native air;
> His watchword at the gates of death;
> He enters heaven with prayer.

From praying Christ eliminates all self-sufficiency, all pride, and all spiritual values. The poor in spirit are the praying ones. Beggars are God's princes. They are God's heirs. Christ removes the rubbish of Jewish traditions and glosses from the regulations of the prayer altar.

> Ye have heard that it was said by them of old time, Thou shalt not kill: and whosoever shall kill shall be in danger of the judgment: But I say unto you, That whosoever is angry with his brother shall be in danger of the judgment: and whosoever shall say to his brother, Raca, shall be in danger of the council: but whosoever shall say, Thou fool, shall be in danger of hell fire. Therefore if thou bring thy gift to the altar,

and there rememberest that thy brother hath ought against
thee: Leave there thy gift before the altar, and go thy way; first
be reconciled to thy brother, and then come and offer thy gift
(Matt. 5:21–24).

He who essays to pray to God with an angry spirit, with
loose and irreverent lips, with an irreconciled heart, and with
unsettled neighborly scores, spends his labor for that which is
worse than naught, violates the law of prayer, and adds to his
sin.

How rigidly exacting is Christ's law of prayer! It goes to the
heart, and demands that love be enthroned there, love to the
brotherhood. The sacrifice of prayer must be seasoned and
perfumed with love, by love in the inward parts. The law of
prayer, its creator and inspirer, is love.

Praying must be done. God wants it done. He commands it.
Man needs it and man must do it. Something must surely
come of praying, for God engages that something shall come
out of it, if men are in earnest and are persevering in prayer.

After Jesus teaches "Ask and it shall be given you," etc., he
encourages real praying, and more praying. He repeats and
avers with redoubled assurance, "For every one that asketh
receiveth." No exception. "Every one." "He that seeketh, findeth." Here it is again, sealed and stamped with infinite veracity.
Then closed and signed, as well as sealed, with divine attesta-
tion, "To him that knocketh it shall be opened." Note how we
are encouraged to pray by our relation to God!

> If ye then, being evil, know how to give good gifts unto your
> children, how much more shall your Father which is in heaven
> give good things to them that ask him? (Matt. 7:11).

The relation of prayer to God's work and God's rule in this
world is most fully illustrated by Jesus Christ in both his
teaching and his practice. He is first in every way and in everything. Among the rulers of the church he is primary in a preeminent way. He has the throne. The golden crown is his in
eminent preciousness. The white garments enrobe him in pre-

eminent whiteness and beauty. In the ministry of prayer he is a divine example as well as the divine teacher. His example is affluent, and his prayer teaching abounds. How imperative the teaching of our Lord when he affirms that "men ought always to pray and not to faint!" and then presents a striking parable of an unjust judge and a poor widow to illustrate and enforce his teaching. It is a necessity to pray. It is exacting and binding for men always to be in prayer. Courage, endurance, and perseverance are demanded that men may never faint in prayer. "And shall not God avenge his own elect that cry day and night unto him?"

This is his strong and indignant questioning and affirmation. Men must pray according to Christ's teaching. They must not get tired nor grow weary in praying. God's character is the assured surety that much will come of the persistent praying of true men.

Doubtless the praying of our Lord had much to do with the revelation made to Peter and the confession he made to Christ, "Thou art the Christ, the Son of the living God." Prayer mightily affects and molds the circle of our associates. Christ made disciples and kept them disciples by praying. His twelve disciples were much impressed by his praying. Never man prayed like this man. How different his praying from the cold, proud, self-righteous praying which they heard and saw on the streets, in the synagogue, and in the temple.

# 6

# Jesus Christ,
# the Divine Teacher of Prayer
# (Continued)

LET it not be forgotten that prayer was one of the great truths which he came into the world to teach and illustrate. It was worth a trip from heaven to earth to teach men this great lesson of prayer. A great lesson it was, a very difficult lesson for men to learn. Men are naturally averse to learning this lesson of prayer. The lesson is a very lowly one. None but God can teach it. It is a despised beggary, a sublime, and heavenly vocation. The disciples were very stupid scholars, but were quickened to prayer by hearing him pray and talk about prayer.

The dispensation of Christ's personality was not, and could not be, the dispensation in its fullest and highest sense of need and dependence. Yet Christ did try to impress on his disciples not alone a deep necessity of the necessity of prayer in general, but also the importance of prayer to them in their personal and spiritual needs. And there came moments to them when they felt the need of a deeper and more thorough schooling in prayer and of their grave neglect in this regard. One of these hours of deep conviction on their part and of eager inquiry was when he was praying at a certain place and time, and they saw him, and they said to him, "Lord, teach us to pray, as John also taught his disciples."

As they listened to him praying, they felt very keenly their ignorance and deficiency in praying. Who has not felt the same deficiency and ignorance? Who has not longed for a teacher in the divine art of praying?

The conviction which these twelve men had of their defect in prayer arose from hearing their Lord and master pray, but likewise from a sense of serious defect even when compared with John the Baptist's training of his disciples in prayer. As they listened to their Lord pray (for unquestionably he must have been seen and heard by them as he prayed, who prayed with marvelous simplicity and power, so human and so divine) such praying had a stimulating charm for them. In the presence and hearing of his praying, very keenly they felt their ignorance and deficiency in prayer. Who has not felt the same ignorance and deficiency?

We do not regret the schooling our Lord gave these twelve men, for in schooling them he schools us. The lesson is one already learned in the law of Christ. But so dull were they, that many a patient emphasis and reiteration was required to instruct them in this divine art of prayer. And likewise so dull are we and inept that many a wearying patient repetition must be given us before we will learn any important lesson in the all-important school of prayer.

This divine teacher of prayer lays himself out to make it clear and strong that God answers prayer, assuredly, certainly, inevitably; that it is the duty of the child to ask, and to press, and that the Father is obliged to answer, and to give for the asking. In Christ's teaching, prayer is no sterile, vain performance, not a mere rite, a form, but a request for an answer, a plea to gain, the seeking of a great good from God. It is a lesson of getting that for which we ask, of finding that for which we seek, and of entering the door at which we knock.

A notable occasion we have as Jesus comes down from the Mount of Transfiguration. He finds his disciples defeated, humiliated, and confused in the presence of their enemies. A father has brought his child possessed with a demon to have the demon cast out. They tried to do it but failed. They had been commissioned by Jesus and sent to do that very work, but had signally failed.

> And when he was come into the house, his disciples asked him privately, saying, Why could not we cast him out? And he said unto them, This kind can come forth by nothing but by prayer and fasting (Mark 9:28–29).

Their faith had not been cultured by prayer. They failed in prayer before they failed in ability to do their work. They failed in faith because they had failed in prayer. That one thing which was necessary to do God's work was prayer. The work which God sends us to do cannot be done without prayer.

In Christ's teaching on prayer we have another pertinent statement. It was in connection with the cursing of the barren fig tree:

> Jesus answered and said unto them, Verily I say unto you, If ye have faith, and doubt not, ye shall not only do this which is done to the fig tree, but also if ye shall say unto this mountain, Be thou removed, and be thou cast into the sea; it shall be done. And all things, whatsoever ye shall ask in prayer, believing, ye shall receive (Matt. 21:21–22).

In this passage we have faith and prayer, their possibilities and powers joined. A fig tree had been blasted to the roots by the word of the Lord Jesus. The power and quickness of the result surprised the disciples. Jesus says to them that it need be no surprise to them or such a difficult work to be done. "If ye have faith" its possibilities to affect will not be confined to the little fig tree, but the gigantic, rock-ribbed, rock-founded mountains can be uprooted and moved into the sea. Prayer is leverage of this great power of faith.

It is well to refer again to the occasion when the heart of our Lord was so deeply moved with compassion as he beheld the multitudes because they fainted and were scattered as having no shepherd. Then it was he urged on his disciples the injunction, "Pray ye the Lord of the harvest that he would send forth laborers into his harvest," clearly teaching them that it belonged to God to call into the ministry men whom he will, and that in answer to prayer the Holy Spirit does this very work.

Prayer is as necessary now as it was then to secure the needed laborers to reap earthly harvests for the heavenly garners. Has the church of God ever learned this lesson of so vital and exacting import? God alone can choose the laborers and thrust them out, and this choosing he does not delegate to man, or church, convocation, synod, association, or conference. And God is moved to this great work of calling men into the ministry by prayer. Earthly fields are rotting. They are untilled because prayer is silent. The laborers are few. Fields are unworked because prayer has not worked with God.

We have the prayer promise and the prayer ability put in a distinct form in the higher teachings of prayer by our Lord: "If ye abide in me, and my words abide in you, ye shall ask what ye will, and it shall be done unto you."

Here we have a fixed attitude of life as the condition of prayer. Not simply a fixed attitude of life toward some great principles or purposes, but the fixed attitude and unity of life with Jesus Christ. To live in him, to dwell there, to be one with him, to draw all life from him, to let all life from him flow through us—this is the attitude of prayer and the ability to pray. No abiding in him can be separated from his Word abiding in us. It must live in us to give birth to and food for prayer. The attitude of the person of Christ is the condition of prayer.

The Old Testament saints had been taught that "God had magnified his word above all his name." New Testament saints must learn fully how to exalt by perfect obedience that Word issuing from the lips of him who is the Word. Praying ones under Christ must learn what praying ones under Moses had already learned, that "man shall not live by bread alone, but by every word that proceedeth out of the mouth of God." The life of Christ flowing through us and the words of Christ living in us, these give potency to prayer. They breathe the spirit of prayer, and make the body, blood, and bones of prayer. Then it is Christ praying in me and through me, and "all things which I will" are the will of

God. My will becomes the law and the answer, for it is written, "Ye shall ask what ye will, and it shall be done unto you."

Our Lord puts fruit bearing to the front in our praying:

> Ye have not chosen me, but I have chosen you, and ordained you, that ye should go and bring forth fruit, and that your fruit shall remain: that whatsoever ye shall ask of the Father in my name, he may give it you (John 15:16).

Barrenness cannot pray. Only fruit-bearing capacity and reality can pray. It is not past fruitfulness, but present: "That your fruit should remain." Fruit, the product of life, is the condition of praying. A life vigorous enough to bear fruit, much fruit, is the condition and the source of prayer.

> And in that day ye shall ask me nothing. Verily, verily, I say unto you, Whatsoever ye shall ask the Father in my name, he will give it you. Hitherto have ye asked nothing in my name: ask, and ye shall receive, that your joy may be full (John 16:23–24).

It is not solving riddles, not revealing mysteries, not curious questionings. This is not our attitude, not our business under the dispensation of the Spirit, but to pray, and to pray largely. Much true praying increases man's joy and God's glory.

"Whatsoever ye shall ask in my name, I will give," says Christ, and the Father will give. Both Father and Son are pledged to give the very things for which we ask. But the condition is in his name. This does not mean that his name is talismanic, to give value by magic. It does not mean that his name in beautiful settings of pearl will give value to prayer. It is not that his name perfumed with sentiment and larded in and closing up our prayers and doings will do the deed. How fearful the statement:

> Many will say to me in that day, Lord, Lord, have we not prophesied in thy name? and in thy name cast out devils? and in thy name done many wonderful works? And then will I profess unto them, I never knew you; depart from me, ye that work iniquity (Matt. 7:22–23).

How blasting the doom of these great workers and doers who claim to work in his name!

It means far more than sentiment, verbiage, and nomenclature. It means to stand in his stead, to bear his nature, to stand for all for which he stood, for righteousness, truth, holiness, and zeal. It means to be one with God as he was, one in spirit, in will, and in purpose. It means that our praying is singly and solely for God's glory through his Son. It means that we abide in him, that Christ prays through us, lives in us and shines out of us; that we pray by the Holy Spirit according to the will of God.

Even amid the darkness of Gethsemane, with the stupor which had settled upon the disciples, we have the sharp warning from Christ to his sluggish disciples, "Watch and pray lest ye enter into temptation. The spirit truly is willing, but the flesh is weak." How needful to hear such a warning, to awaken all our powers, not simply for the great crises of our lives, but as the inseparable and constant attendants of a career marked with perils and dangers on every hand.

As Christ nears the close of his earthly mission, nearer to the greater and more powerful dispensation of the Spirit, his teaching about prayer takes on a more absorbing and higher form. It has now become a graduating school. His connection with prayer becomes more intimate and more absolute. He becomes in prayer what he is in all else pertaining to our salvation, the beginning and the end, the first and the last. His name becomes all potent. Mighty works are to be done by the faith which can pray in his name. Like his nature, his name covers all needs, embraces all worlds, and gets all good.

> Believest thou not that I am in the Father, and the Father in me? The words that I speak unto you I speak not of myself: but the Father that dwelleth in me, he doeth the works. Believe me that I am in the Father, and the Father in me: or else believe me for the very works' sake. Verily, verily, I say unto you, He that believeth on me, the works that I do shall he do also; and greater works than these shall he do; because I go unto my Father. And whatsoever ye shall ask in my name, that will I do, that the Father

may be glorified in the Son. If ye shall ask any thing in my name, I will do it (John 14:10–14).

The Father, the Son, and the praying one are all bound up together. All things are in Christ, and all things are in prayer in his name. "If ye shall ask anything in my name." The key which unlocks the vast storehouse of God is prayer. The power to do greater works than Christ did lies in the faith which can grasp his name truly and in true praying.

In the last of his life, note how he urges prayer as a preventive of the many evils to which they were exposed. In view of the temporal and fearful terrors of the destruction of Jerusalem, he charges them to this effect: "Pray ye that your flight be not in winter."

How many evils in this life which can be escaped by prayer! How many fearful temporal calamities can be mitigated, if not wholly relieved, by prayer! Notice how, amid the excesses and stupefying influences to which we are exposed in this world, Christ charges us to pray:

And take heed to yourselves, lest at any time your hearts be overcharged with surfeiting, and drunkenness, and cares of this life, and so that day come upon you unawares. For as a snare shall it come on all them that dwell on the face of the whole earth. Watch ye therefore, and pray always, that ye may be accounted worthy to escape all these things that shall come to pass, and to stand before the Son of man (Luke 21:34–36).

In view of the uncertainty of Christ's coming to judgment, and the uncertainty of our going out of this world, he says:

But of that day and that hour knoweth no man, no, not the angels which are in heaven, neither the Son, but the Father. Take ye heed, watch and pray: for ye know not when the time is (Mark 13:32–33).

We have the words of Jesus as given in his last interview with his twelve disciples, found in the Gospel of John, chapters fourteen to seventeen, inclusive. These are true, solemn parting words. The disciples were to move out into the regions of toil and peril, bereft of the personal presence of their Lord and master. They were to be impressed that prayer would serve them in everything, and its use, and unlimited possibilities would in some measure supply their loss, and by it they would be able to command all the possibilities of Jesus Christ and God the Father.

It was the occasion of momentous interest to Jesus Christ. His work was to receive its climax and crown in his death and his resurrection. His glory and the success of his work and of its execution, under the mastery and direction of the Holy Spirit, was to be committed to his apostles. To them it was an hour of strange wonderment and of peculiar, mysterious sorrow, only too well assured of the fact that Jesus was to leave them. Dark and impalpable was all else.

He was to give them his parting words and pray his parting prayer. Solemn, vital truths were to be the weight and counsel of that hour. He speaks to them of heaven. Young men, strong though they were, yet they could not meet the duties of their preaching life and their apostolic life, without the fact, the thought, the hope, and the relish of heaven. These things were to be present constantly in all sweetness, in all their vigor, in all freshness, in all brightness. He spoke to them about their spiritual and conscious connection with himself, an abiding indwelling, so close and continuous that his own life would flow into them, as the life of the vine flows into the branches. Their lives and their fruitfulness were dependent on this. Then praying was urged on them as one of the vital, essential forces. This was the one thing upon which all the divine force depended, and this was the avenue and agency through which the divine life and power were to be secured and continued in their ministry.

He spoke to them about prayer. He had taught them many lessons upon this all-important subject as they had been together. This solemn hour he seizes to perfect his teaching. They must be made to realize that they have an illimitable and exhaustless storehouse of good in God and that they can draw on him at all times and for all things without stint, as Paul said in later years to the Philippians, "My God shall supply all your need according to his riches in glory by Christ Jesus."

# 7

## Jesus Christ, an Example of Prayer

THE Bible record of the life of Jesus Christ gives but a glance of his busy doing, a small selection of his many words, and only a brief record of his great works. But even in this record we see him as being much in prayer. Even though busy and exhausted by the severe strain and toils of his life, "in the morning a great while before day, he rose up and went out and departed into a desert place, and there prayed." Alone in the desert and in the darkness with God! Prayer filled the life of our Lord while on earth. His life was a constant stream of incense sweet and perfumed by prayer. When we see how the life of Jesus was but one of prayer, then we must conclude that to be like Jesus is to pray like Jesus and is to live like Jesus. A serious life it is to pray as Jesus prayed.

We cannot follow any chronological order in the praying of Jesus Christ. What were his steps of advance and skill in the divine art of praying we know not. He is in the act of prayer when we find him at the fords of the Jordan, when the waters of baptism, at the hands of John the Baptist, are on him. So passing over the three years of his ministry, when closing the drama of his life in that terrible baptism of fear, pain, suffering, and shame, we find him in the spirit, and also in the very act of praying. The baptism of the cross, as well as the baptism of the Jordan, are sanctified by prayer. With the breath of prayer in his last sigh, he commits his spirit to God. In his first recorded utterances, as well as his first acts, we find him teaching his disciples how to pray as his first lesson, and as their first duty. Under the shadow of the cross, in the urgency and importance of his last interview with his chosen disciples, he is at the same all-important business, teaching the world's teachers how to pray, trying to make prayerful those lips and hearts out of which were to flow the divine deposits of truth.

The great eras of his life were created and crowned with prayer. What were his habits of prayer during his stay at home and his toil as a carpenter in Nazareth, we have no means of knowing. God has veiled it, and guess and speculation are not only vain and misleading, but proud and prurient. It would be presumptuous searching into that which God has hidden, which would make us seek to be wise above that which was written, trying to lift up the veil with which God has covered his own revelation.

We find Christ in the presence of the famed, the prophet and the preacher. He has left his Nazareth home and his carpenter shop by God's call. He is now at a transitional point. He has moved out to his great work. John's baptism and the baptism of the Holy Spirit are prefatory and are to qualify him for that work. This epochal and transitional period is marked by prayer.

> Now when all the people were baptized, it came to pass that Jesus, also being baptized, and praying, the heaven was opened, And the Holy Ghost descended in a bodily shape like a dove upon him, and a voice came from heaven, which said, thou art my beloved Son; in thee I am well pleased (Luke 3:21–22).

It is a supreme hour in his history, different and in striking contrast with, but not in opposition to, the past. The descent and abiding of the Holy Spirit in all his fullness, the opening heavens, and the attesting voice which involved God's recognition of his only Son—all these are the result, if not the direct creation and response to his praying on that occasion.

"As he was praying," so we are to be praying. If we would pray as Christ prayed, we must be as Christ was, and must live as Christ lived. The Christ character, the Christ life, and the Christ spirit, must be ours if we would do the Christ praying, and would have our prayers answered as he had his prayers answered. The business of Christ even now in heaven at his Father's right hand is to pray. Certainly if we are his, if we love him, if we live for him, and if we live close to him, we will catch the contagion of his praying life, both on earth and in heaven. We will learn his trade and carry on his business on earth.

Jesus Christ loved all men, he tasted death for all men, he intercedes for all men. Let us ask then, are we the imitators, the representatives, and the executors of Jesus Christ? Then must we in our prayers run parallel with his atonement in its extent. The atoning blood of Jesus Christ gives sanctity and efficiency to our prayers. As worldwide, as broad, and as human as the man Christ Jesus was, so must be our prayers. The intercessions of Christ's people must give currency and expedition to the work of Christ, carry the atoning blood to its beneficial ends, and help to strike off the chains of sin from every ransomed soul. We must be as praying, as tearful, and as compassionate as was Christ.

Prayer affects all things. God blesses the person who prays. He who prays goes out on a long voyage for God and is enriched himself while enriching others, and is blessed himself while the world is blessed by his praying. "To live a quiet and peaceable life in all godliness and honesty" is the wealthiest wealth.

The praying of Christ was real. No man prayed as he prayed. Prayer pressed upon him as a solemn, all-imperative, all-commanding duty, as well as a royal privilege in which all sweetness was condensed, alluring, and absorbing. Prayer was the secret of his power, the law of his life, the inspiration of his toil and the source of his wealth, his joy, his communion, and his strength.

To Christ Jesus prayer occupied no secondary place, but was exacting and paramount, a necessity, a life, the satisfying of a restless yearning and a preparation for heavy responsibilities.

Closeting with his Father in counsel and fellowship, with vigor and in deep joy, all this was his praying. Present trials, future glory, the history of his church, and the struggles and perils of his disciples in all times and to the very end of time, all these things were born and shaped by his praying.

Nothing is more conspicuous in the life of our Lord than prayer. His campaigns were arranged and his victories were gained in the struggles and communion of his all-night praying. By prayer he rent the heavens. Moses and Elijah and the transfiguration glory wait on his praying. His miracles and teaching had their power from the same source. Gethsemane's praying crimsoned Calvary with serenity and glory. His high-priestly prayer makes the history and hastens the triumph of his church on earth. What an inspiration and command to pray is the prayer life of Jesus Christ while in this world! What a comment it is on the value, the nature, and the necessity of prayer!

The dispensation of the person of Jesus Christ was a dispensation of prayer. A synopsis of his teaching and practice of prayer was that "Men ought always to pray and not to faint."

As the Jews prayed in the name of their patriarchs and invoked the privileges granted to them by covenant with God; as we have a new name and a new covenant, more privileged and more powerful and more all-comprehensive, more authoritative and more divine; and as far as the Son of God is lifted above the patriarchs in divinity, glory, and power, by so much should our praying exceed theirs in range of largeness, glory, and power of results.

Jesus Christ prayed to God as Father. Simply and directly did he approach God in the charmed and revered circle of the Father. The awful, repelling fear was entirely absent, lost in the supreme confidence of a child.

Jesus Christ crowns his life, his works, and his teaching with prayer. How his Father attests his relationship and puts on him the glory of answered prayer at his baptism and transfiguration when all other glories are growing dim in the night which settles on him! What almighty potencies are in prayer when we are charged and surcharged with but one inspiration and aim! "Father, glorify thy name." This sweetens all, brightens all, conquers all, and gets all. Father, glorify thy name." That guiding star will illumine the darkest night and calm the wildest storm and will make us brave and true. An imperial principle it is. It will make an imperial Christian.

The range and potencies of prayer, so clearly shown by Jesus in life and teaching, but reveal the great purposes of God. They not only reveal the Son in the reality and fullness of his humanity, but also reveal the Father.

Christ prayed as a child. The spirit of a child was found in him. At the grave of Lazarus "Jesus lifted up his eyes and said, 'Father.'" Again we hear him begin his prayer after this fashion: "In that hour Jesus rejoiced in spirit, and said, 'I thank thee, O Father.'" So also on other occasions we find him in prayer addressing God as his Father, assuming the attitude of the child asking something of the Father. What confidence, simplicity, and artlessness! What readiness, freeness, and fullness of approach are all involved in the spirit of a child! What confiding trust, what assurance, what tender interest! What profound solicitudes and tender sympathy on the Father's part! What respect deepening into reverence! What loving obedience and grateful emotions glow in the child's heart! What divine fellowship and royal intimacy! What sacred and sweet emotions! All these meet in the hour of prayer when the child of God meets his Father in heaven, and when the Father meets his child! We must live as children if we would ask as children. We must act as children if we would pray as children. The spirit of prayer is born of the child spirit.

The profound reverence in this relation of paternity must forever exclude all lightness, frivolity, and pertness, as well as all undue familiarity. Solemnity and gravity become the hour of prayer. It has been well said: "The worshiper who invokes God under the name of Father and realizes the gracious and beneficent love of God must at the same time remember and recognize God's glorious majesty, which is neither annulled nor impaired, but rather supremely intensified through his fatherly love. An appeal to God as Father, if not associated with reverence and homage before the divine majesty, would betray a want of understanding of the character of God." And, we might add, would show a lack of the attributes of a child.

Patriarchs and prophets knew something of the doctrine of the fatherhood of God to God's family. They "saw it afar off, were persuaded of it, and embraced it," but understood it not, in all its fullness, "God having provided some better thing for us, that they without us should not be made perfect."

"Behold he prayeth!" was God's response, to the wonderment and surprise of the timid Ananias, in regard to Saul of Tarsus. "Behold he prayeth!" applied to Christ has in it far more of wonderment and mystery and surprise. He, the maker of all worlds, the Lord of angels and of men, co-equal and co-eternal with the everlasting God; the "brightness of the Father's glory and the express image of his person"; "fresh from his Father's glory and from his Father's throne." "Behold he prayeth!" To find him in lowly, dependent attitude of prayer, the suppliant of all suppliants, his richest legacy and his royal privilege to pray—this is the mystery of all mysteries, the wonder of all wonders.

Hebrews 5:7 gives in brief and comprehensive statement the habit of our Lord in prayer—"Who in the days of his flesh, when he had offered up prayers and supplications with strong crying and tears unto him that was able to save him from death, and was heard in that he feared." We have in this description of our Lord's praying the outgoing of great spiritual forces. He prayed with "prayers and supplications." It was no formal, tentative effort. He was intense, personal, and real. He was a pleader for God's good. He was in great need and he must cry with "strong cryings," made stronger still by his tears. In an agony the Son of God wrestled. His praying was no playing a mere part. His soul was engaged, and all his powers were taxed to a strain. Let us pause and look at him and learn how to pray in earnest. Let us learn how to win in an agony of prayer that which seems to be withheld from us. A beautiful word is that, "feared," which occurs only twice in the New Testament, the fear of God.

Jesus Christ was always a busy man with his work, but never too busy to pray. The divinest of business filled his heart and filled his hands, consumed his time, exhausted his nerves. But with him even God's work must not crowd out God's praying. Saving people from sin or suffering must not, even with Christ, be substituted for praying, nor abate in the least the time or the intensity of these holiest of seasons. He filled the day with working for God; he employed the night with praying to God. The day-working made the night-praying a necessity. The night-praying sanctified and made successful the day-working. Too busy to pray gives religion Christian burial, it is true, but kills it nevertheless.

In many cases only the bare fact, yet important and suggestive fact, is stated that he prayed. In other cases the very words which came out of his heart and fell from his lips are recorded. The man of prayer by preeminence was Jesus Christ. The epochs of his life were created by prayer, and all the minor details, outlines, and forms of his life were inspired, colored, and impregnated by prayer. The prayer words of Jesus were sacred words.

By them God speaks to God, and by them God is revealed and prayer is illustrated and enforced. Here is prayer in its purest form and in its mightiest potencies. It would seem that earth and heaven would uncover head and open ears most wide to catch the words of his praying who was truest God and truest man, and divinest of suppliants, who prayed as never man prayed. His prayers are our inspiration and pattern to pray.

# 8

# Prayer Incidents
# in the Life of Our Lord

ONE of Christ's most impassioned and sublime paeans of prayer and praise is recorded by both Matthew and Luke, with small verbal contrasts and with some diversity of detail and environments. He is reviewing the poor results of his ministry and remarking upon the feeble responses of man to God's vast outlay of love and mercy. He is arraigning the ingratitude of men to God, and is showing the fearfully destructive results of their indifference with their increased opportunities, favors, and responsibilities.

In the midst of these arraignments, denunciations, and woes, the seventy disciples return to report the results of their mission. They were full of exhilaration at their success, and evinced it with no little self-gratulation. The spirit of Jesus was diverted, relieved, and refreshed by their animation, catching somewhat the contagion of their joy, and sharing in their triumph. He rejoiced, gave thanks, and prayed a prayer wonderful for its brevity, its inspiration, and its revelation:

> In that hour Jesus rejoiced in spirit, and said, I thank thee, O Father, Lord of heaven and earth, that thou hast hid these things from the wise and prudent, and hast revealed them unto

61

babes: even so, Father; for so it seemed good in thy sight. All
things are delivered to me of my Father; and no man knoweth
who the Son is, but the Father; and who the Father is, but the
Son, and he to whom the Son will reveal him (Luke 10:21–22).

The Christ life was in the image of his Father. He was the
"express image of his person." And so the spirit of prayer with
Christ was to do God's will. His constant assertion was that he
"came to do his Father's will," and not his own will. When the
fearful crisis came in his life in Gethsemane, and all its darkness, direness, and dread, with the crushing weight of man's
sins and sorrows which were pressing down upon him, his
spirit and frame crushed, and almost expiring, then he cried
out for relief, yet it was not his will which was to be followed.
It was only an appeal out of weakness and death for God's
relief in God's way. God's will was to be the law and the rule of
his relief, if relief came.

So he who follows Christ in prayer must have God's will as
his law, his rule, and his inspiration. In all praying, it is the
man who prays. The life and the character flow into the closet.
There is a mutual action and reaction. The closet has much to
do with making the character, while the character has much to
do with making the closet. It is "the effectual fervent prayer of
the righteous man which availeth much." It is with them who
"call upon the Lord out of a pure heart" we are to consort.
Christ was the greatest of pray-ers because he was the holiest
of men. His character is the praying character. His spirit is the
life and power of prayer. He is not the best pray-er who has the
greatest fluency, the most brilliant imagination, the richest
gifts, and the most fiery ardor, but he who has imbibed most of
the spirit of Christ.

It is he whose character is the nearest to a facsimile of
Christ upon whom God's power is bestowed and to whom
God's person and will are revealed. "Hid these things from the
wise and prudent," those, for instance, who are wise in their
own eyes, skilled in letters, cultured, learned, philosophers,
scribes, doctors, rabbis. "Prudent"—one who can put things
together, having insight, comprehension, expression. God's

revelation of himself and his will cannot be sought out and understood by reason, intelligence, or great learning. Great men and great minds are neither the channels nor depositories of God's revelation by virtue of their culture, braininess, nor wisdom. God's system in redemption and providence is not to be thought out, open only to the learned and wise. The learned and the wise, following their learning and their wisdom, have always sadly and darkly missed God's thoughts and God's ways.

The condition of receiving God's revelation and of holding God's truth is one of the heart, not one of the head. The ability to receive and search out is like that of the child, the babe, the synonym of docility, innocence, and simplicity. These are the conditions on which God reveals himself to men. The world by wisdom cannot know God. The world by wisdom can never receive nor understand God, because God reveals himself to men's hearts, not to their heads. Only hearts can ever know God, can feel God, can see God, and can read God in his book of books. God is not grasped by thought but by feeling. The world gets God by revelation, not by philosophy. It is not apprehension, the mental ability to grasp God, but plasticity, ability to be impressed, that men need. It is not by hard, strong, stern, great reasoning that the world gets God or gets hold of God, but by big, soft, pure hearts. Not so much do men need light to see God as they need hearts to feel God.

Human wisdom, great natural talents, and the culture of the schools, howsoever good they may be, can neither be the repositories nor conservers of God's revealed truth. The tree of knowledge has been the bane of faith, ever essaying to reduce revelation to a philosophy and to measure God by man. In its pride, it puts God out and puts man into God's truth. To become babes again, on our mother's bosom, quieted, weaned, without clamor or protest, is the only position in which to know God. A calmness on the surface, and in the depths of the soul, in which God can mirror his will, his Word and himself—this is the attitude toward him through which he can reveal himself, and this attitude is the right attitude of prayer.

Our Lord taught us the lesson of prayer by putting into practice in his life what he taught by his lips. Here is a simple but important statement, full of meaning: "And when he had sent the multitudes away, he went up into a mountain apart to pray: and when the evening was come he was there alone."

The multitudes had been fed and were dismissed by our Lord.

The divine work of healing and teaching must be stayed awhile in order that time, place, and opportunity for prayer might be secured—prayer, the divinest of all labor, the most important of all ministries. Away from the eager, anxious, seeking multitudes, he has gone while the day is yet bright, to be alone with God. The multitudes tax and exhaust him. The disciples are tossed on the sea, but calmness reigns on the mountain top where our Lord is kneeling in secret prayer— where prayer rules. "When Jesus therefore perceived that they would come and take him by force, to make him a king, he departed again into a mountain alone."

He must be alone in that moment with God. Temptation was in that hour. The multitude had feasted on the five loaves and the two fishes. Filled with food and excited beyond measure, they would fain make him king. He flees from the temptation to secret prayer, for here is the source of his strength to resist evil. What a refuge was secret prayer even to him! What a refuge to us from the world's dazzling and delusive crowns! What safety there is to be alone with God when the world tempts us, allures us, attracts us!

The prayers of our Lord are prophetic and illustrative of the great truth that the greatest measure of the Holy Spirit, the attesting voice and opening heavens are only secured by prayer. This is suggested by his baptism by John the Baptist, when he prayed as he was baptized, and immediately the Holy Spirit descended upon him like a dove. More than prophetic and illustrative is this hour to him. This critical hour is real and personal, consecrating and qualifying him for God's highest purposes. Prayer to him, just as it is to us, was a necessity, an absolute, invariable condition of securing God's fullest, consecrating and qualifying power. The Holy Spirit came upon him in fullness of measure and power in the very act of prayer.

And so the Holy Spirit comes upon us in fullness of measure and power only in answer to ardent and intense praying. The heavens were opened to Christ, and access and communion established and enlarged by prayer. Freedom and fullness of access and closeness of communion are secured to us as the heritage of prayer. The voice attesting his sonship came to Christ in prayer. The witness of our sonship, clear and indubitable, is secured only by praying. The constant witness of our sonship can only be retained by those who pray without ceasing. When the stream of prayer is shallow and arrested, the evidence of our sonship becomes faint and inaudible.

# 9

# Prayer Incidents
in the Life of Our Lord
(*Continued*)

WE note that from the revelation and inspiration of a transporting prayer-hour of Christ, as its natural sequence, there sounds out that gracious encouraging proclamation for heavy-hearted, restless, weary souls of earth, which has so impressed, arrested, and drawn humanity as it has fallen on the ears of heavy-laden souls, which has so sweetened and relieved men of their toils and burdens:

> Come unto me, all ye that labor and are heavy laden, and I will give you rest. Take my yoke upon you, and learn of me; for I am meek and lowly in heart: and ye shall find rest unto your souls. For my yoke is easy, and my burden is light (Matt. 11:28–30).

At the grave of Lazarus and as preparatory to and as a condition of calling him back to life, we have our Lord calling upon his Father in heaven. "Father, I thank thee that thou hast heard me, and I knew that thou hearest me always." The lifting to heaven of Christ's eyes—how much was there in it! How much of confidence and plea was in that look to heaven! His very look, the lifting up of his eyes, carried his whole being heavenward, and caused a pause in that world, and drew attention and help. All heaven was engaged, pledged, and moved when the Son of God looked up at this grave. O for a people with the Christlike eye, heaven lifted and heaven arresting! As it was with Christ, so ought we to be so perfected in faith, so skilled in praying, that we could lift our eyes to heaven and say with him, with deepest humility, and with commanding confidence, "Father, I thank thee that thou hast heard me."

Once more we have a very touching and beautiful and instructive incident in Christ's praying, this time having to do with infants in their mothers' arms, parabolic as well as historical:

> Then were there brought unto him little children, that he should put his hands on them, and pray: and the disciples rebuked them. . . . But when Jesus saw it, he was much displeased, and said unto them, Suffer the little children to come unto me, and forbid them not; for of such is the kingdom of God. Verily I say unto you, whosoever shall not receive the kingdom of God as a little child, he shall not enter therein. And he took them up in his arms, put his hands upon them, and blessed them (Matt. 19:13; Mark 10:14–16).

This was one of the few times when stupid ignorance and unspiritual views aroused his indignation and displeasure. Vital principles were involved. The foundations were being destroyed, and worldly views actuated the disciples. Their temper and their words in rebuking those who brought their infants to Christ were exceedingly wrong. The very principles which he came to illustrate and propagate were being violated. Christ received the little ones. The big ones must become little ones. The old ones must become young ones ere Christ will receive them. Prayer helps the little ones. The cradle must be invested with prayer. We are to pray for our little ones. The children are now to be brought to Jesus Christ by prayer, as he is in heaven and not on earth. They are to be brought to him early for his blessing, even when they are infants. His blessing descends upon these little ones in answer to the prayers of those who bring them. With untiring importunity are they to be brought to Christ in earnest, persevering prayer by their fathers and mothers. Before they know anything about coming of their own accord, parents are to present them to God in prayer, seeking his blessing upon their offspring and at the same time asking for wisdom, grace, and divine help to rear them that they may come to Christ when they arrive at the years of accountability of their own accord.

Holy hands and holy praying have much to do with guarding and training young lives and to form young characters for righteousness and heaven. What graciousness, simplicity, kindness, unworldliness, condescension, and meekness, linked with prayerfulness, are in this act of this divine teacher!

It was as Jesus was praying that Peter made that wonderful confession of his faith that Jesus was the Son of God:

> And it came to pass, as he was alone praying, his disciples were with him: and he asked them, saying, Whom say the people that I am? . . . And they said, Some say that thou art John the Baptist; some, Elias; and others, Jeremias or one of the prophets. He saith unto them, But whom say ye that I am? And Simon Peter answered and said, Thou art the Christ, the Son of the living God. And Jesus answered and said unto him, Blessed art thou, Simon Bar-jona; for flesh and blood hath not revealed it unto thee, but my Father which is in heaven. And I say also unto thee, that thou art Peter, and upon this rock I will build my church: and the gates of hell shall not prevail against it. And I will give unto thee the keys of the kingdom of heaven; and whatsoever thou shalt bind on earth shall be bound in heaven; and whatsoever thou shalt loose on earth shall be loosed in heaven (Luke 9:18; Matt. 16:14–19).

It was after our Lord had made large promises to his disciples that he had appointed unto each of them a kingdom, and that they should sit at his table in his kingdom and sit on thrones judging the twelve tribes of Israel, that he gave those words of warning to Simon Peter, telling him that he had prayed for Peter.

And the Lord said, Simon, Simon, behold Satan hath desired
to have you, so that he may sift you as wheat. But I have prayed
for thee, that thy faith fail not: and when thou art converted,
strengthen thy brethren (Luke 22:31–32).

Happy Peter, to have such a one as the Son of God to pray
for him! Unhappy Peter, to be so in the toils of Satan as to
demand so much of Christ's solicitude! How intense are the
demands upon our prayers for some specific cases! Prayer
must be personal to be to the fullest extent beneficial. Peter
drew on Christ's praying more than any other disciple
because of his exposure to greater perils. Pray for the most
impulsive, the most imperiled ones by name. Our love and
their danger give frequency, inspiration, intensity, and personality to praying.

We have seen how Christ had to flee from the multitude
after the magnificent miracle of feeding the five thousand as
they sought to make him king. Then prayer was his escape and
his refuge from this strong worldly temptation. He returns
from that night of prayer with strength and calmness, and with
a power to perform that other remarkable miracle of great
wonder of walking on the sea.

Even the loaves and fishes were sanctified by prayer before
he served them to the multitude. "He looked up to heaven and
gave thanks." Prayer should sanctify our daily bread and mul-
tiply our seed sown.

He looked up to heaven and heaved a sigh when he touched
the tongue of the deaf man who had an impediment in his
speech. Much akin was this sigh to that groaning in spirit
which he evinced at the grave of Lazarus. "Jesus therefore
again groaning in himself, cometh to the grave." Here was the
sigh and groan of the Son of God over a human wreck, groaning that sin and hell had such a mastery over man; troubled
that such a desolation and ruin were man's sad inheritance.
This is a lesson to be ever learned by us. Here is a fact ever to
be kept in mind and heart and which must ever, in some measure, weigh upon the inner spirits of God's children. We who
have received the first fruit of the Spirit groan within ourselves

at sin's waste, and death, and are filled with longings for the coming of a better day.

Present in all great praying, making and marking it, is the man. It is impossible to separate the praying from the man. The constituent elements of the man are the constituents of his praying. The man flows through his praying. Only the fiery Elijah could do Elijah's fiery praying. We can get holy praying only from a holy man. Holy being can never exist without holy doing. Being is first, doing comes afterward. What we are gives being, force, and inspiration to what we do. Character, that which is graven deep, ineradicably, imperishably within us, colors all we do.

The praying of Christ, then, is not to be separated from the character of Christ. If he prayed more unweariedly, more self-denyingly, more holily, more simply and directly than other men, it was because these elements entered more largely into his character than into that of others.

The transfiguration marks another epoch in his life, and that was preeminently a prayer epoch. Luke gives an account with the purpose and aim of the event:

> And it came to pass about an eight days after these sayings, he took Peter and John and James, and went up into a mountain to pray. And as he prayed, the fashion of his countenance was altered, and his raiment was white and glistering. And, behold, there talked with him two men, which were Moses and Elias: Who appeared in glory, and spake of his decease which he should accomplish at Jerusalem (Luke 9:28–31).

The selection was made of three of his disciples for an inner circle of associates, in prayer. Few there be who have the spiritual tastes or aptitude for this inner circle. Even these three favored ones could scarcely stand the strain of that long night of praying. We know that he went up on that mountain to pray, not to be transfigured. But it was as he prayed, the fashion of his countenance was altered and his raiment became white and glistering. There is nothing like prayer to change character and whiten conduct. There is nothing like prayer to bring heavenly visitants and to gild with heavenly glory earth's mountain to us, dull and drear. Peter calls it the holy mount, made so by prayer.

Three times did the voice of God bear witness to the presence and person of his Son, Jesus Christ—at his baptism by John the Baptist, and then at his transfiguration the approving, consoling, and witnessing voice of his Father was heard. He was found in prayer both of these times. The third time the attesting voice came, it was not on the heights of his transfigured glory, nor was it as he was girding himself to begin his conflict and to enter upon his ministry, but it was when he was hastening to the awful end. He was entering the dark mystery of his last agony, and looking forward to it. The shadows were deepening, a dire calamity was approaching and an unknown and untried dread was before him. Ruminating on his approaching death, prophesying about it, and forecasting the glory which would follow, in the midst of his high and mysterious discourse, the shadows come like a dread eclipse and he bursts out in an agony of prayer:

> Now is my soul troubled; and what shall I say? Father, save me from this hour: but for this cause came I unto this hour. Father, glorify thy name. Then came there a voice from heaven, saying, I have both glorified it, and will glorify it again. The people therefore that stood by, and heard it, said that it thundered: others said, An angel spake to him. Jesus answered and said, This voice came not because of me, but for your sakes (John 12:27–30).

But let it be noted that Christ is meeting and illuminating this fateful and distressing hour with prayer. How even thus early the flesh reluctantly shrank from the contemplated end!

How fully does his prayer on the cross for his enemies synchronize with all he taught about love to our enemies, and with mercy and forgiveness to those who have trespassed against us! "Then said Jesus, Father, forgive them; for they know not what they do." Apologizing for his murderers and praying for them, while they were jeering and mocking him at his death pains and their hands were reeking with his blood! What amazing generosity, pity, and love!

Again, take another one of the prayers on the cross. How touching the prayer and how bitter the cup! How dark and desolate the hour as he exclaims, "My God, my God, why hast thou forsaken me?" This is the last stroke that rends in twain his heart, more exquisite in its bitterness and its anguish and more heart-piercing than the kiss of Judas. All else was looked for, all else was put in his book of sorrows. But to have his Father's face withdrawn, God-forsaken, the hour when these distressing words escaped the lips of the dying Son of God! And yet how truthful he is! How childlike we find him! And so when the end really comes, we hear him again speaking to his Father: "Father, into thy hands I commit my spirit. And having said this, he gave up the ghost."

# 10

# Our Lord's Model Prayer

JESUS gives us the pattern prayer in what is commonly known as "The Lord's Prayer." In this model, perfect prayer he gives us a law form to be followed, and yet one to be filled in and enlarged as we may decide when we pray. The outlines and form are complete, yet it is but an outline, with many a blank, which our needs and convictions are to fill in.

Christ puts words on our lips, words which are to be uttered by holy lives. Words belong to the life of prayer. Wordless prayers are like human spirits; pure and high they may be, but too ethereal and impalpable for earthly conflicts and earthly needs and uses. We must have spirits clothed in flesh and blood, and our prayers must be likewise clothed in words to give them point and power, a local habitation, and a name.

This lesson of The Lord's Prayer, drawn forth by the request of the disciples, "Lord, teach us to pray," has something in form and verbiage like the prayer sections of the Sermon on the Mount. It is the same great lesson of praying to "Our Father which art in heaven," and is one of insistent importunity. No prayer lesson would be complete without it. It belongs to the first and last lessons in prayer. God's fatherhood gives shape, value, and confidence to all our praying.

He teaches us that to hallow God's name is the first and the greatest of prayers. A desire for the glorious coming and the glorious establishment of God's glorious kingdom follows in value and in sequence the hallowing of God's name. He who really hallows God's name will hail the coming of the kingdom of God, and will labor and pray to bring that kingdom to pass and to establish it. Christ's pupils in the school of prayer are to be taught diligently to hallow God's name, to work for God's kingdom, and to do God's will perfectly, completely, and gladly, as it is done in heaven.

Prayer engages the highest interest and secures the highest glory of God. God's name, God's kingdom, and God's will are all in it. Without prayer his name is profaned, his kingdom fails, and his will is decried and opposed. God's will can be done on earth as it is done in heaven. God's will done on earth makes earth like heaven. Importunate praying is the mighty energy which establishes God's will on earth as it is established in heaven.

He is still teaching us that prayer sanctifies and makes hopeful and sweet our daily toil for daily bread. Forgiveness of sins is to be sought by prayer, and the great prayer plea we are to make for forgiveness is that we have forgiven all those who have sinned against us. It involves love for our enemies so far as to pray for them, to bless them and not curse them, and to pardon their offenses against us whatever those offenses may be.

We are to pray, "Lead us not into temptation," that is, that while we thus pray, the tempter and the temptation are to be watched against, resisted, and prayed against.

All these things he had laid down in this law of prayer, but many a simple lesson of comment, expansion, and expression he adds to his statute law.

In this prayer he teaches his disciples, so familiar to thousands in this day who learned it at their mother's knees in childhood, the words are so childlike that children find their instruction, edification, and comfort in them as they kneel and pray. The most glowing mystic and the most careful thinker finds his own language in these simple words of prayer. Beautiful and revered as these words are, they are our words for solace, help, and learning.

He led the way in prayer that we might follow his footsteps. Matchless leader in matchless praying! Lord, teach us to pray as thou didst thyself pray!

How marked the contrast between the high-priestly prayer and this "Lord's Prayer," this copy for praying he gave to his disciples as the first elements of prayer. How simple and child-like! No one has ever approached in composition a prayer so simple in its petitions and yet so comprehensive in all of its requests.

How these simple elements of prayer as given by our Lord commend themselves to us! This prayer is for us as well as for those to whom it was first given. It is for the child in the ABCs of prayer, and it is for the graduate of the highest institutions of learning. It is a personal prayer, reaching to all our needs and covering all our sins. It is the highest form of prayer for others. As the scholar can never in all his after studies or learning dispense with his ABCs, and as the alphabet gives form, color, and expression to all after learning, impregnating all, and grounding all, so the learner in Christ can never dispense with the Lord's Prayer. But he may make it form the basis of his higher praying, this intercession for others in the high-priestly prayer.

The Lord's Prayer is ours by our mother's knee and fits us in all the stages of a joyous Christian life. The high-priestly prayer is ours also in the stages and office of our royal priesthood as intercessors before God. Here we have oneness with God, deep spiritual unity, and unswerving loyalty to God, living and praying to glorify God.

# 11

## Our Lord's High-Priestly Prayer

WE come now to consider our Lord's high-priestly prayer, as found recorded in the seventeenth chapter of John's Gospel.

Obedience to the Father and abiding in the Father, these belong to the Son, and these belong to us, as partners with Christ in his divine work of intercession. How tenderly and with what pathos and how absorbingly he prays for his disciples! "I pray for them; I pray not for the world." What a pattern of prayerfulness for God's people! For God's people are God's cause, God's church, and God's kingdom. Pray for God's people, for their unity, their sanctification, and their glorification. How the subject of their unity pressed upon him! These walls of separation, these alienations, these riven circles of God's family, and these warring tribes of ecclesiastics—how he is torn and bleeds and suffers afresh at the sight of these divisions! Unity—that is the great burden of that remarkable high-priestly prayer. "That they may be one, even as we are one." The spiritual oneness of God's people—that is the heritage of God's glory to them, transmitted by Christ to his church.

First of all, in this prayer, Jesus prays for himself, not now the suppliant as in Gethsemane, not weakness, but strength now. There is not now the pressure of darkness and of hell, but passing for the time over the fearful interim, he asks that he may be glorified, and that his exalted glory may secure glory to his Father. His sublime loyalty and fidelity to God are declared, that fidelity to God which is of the very essence of interceding prayer. Our devoted lives pray. Our unswerving loyalty to God are eloquent pleas to him, and give access and confidence in our advocacy. This prayer is gemmed, but its walls are adamant. What profound and granite truths! What fathomless mysteries! What deep and rich experiences do such statements as these involve:

> And this is life eternal, that they might know thee the only true God, and Jesus Christ, whom thou hast sent. And all mine are thine, and thine are mine, and I am glorified in them. And I have declared unto them thy name, and will declare it, that the love wherewith thou hast loved me may be in them, and I in them. And now, O Father, glorify thou me with thine own self with the glory which I had with thee before the world was (John 17:3, 10, 26, 5).

Let us stop and ask, have we eternal life? Do we know God experimentally, consciously, and do we know him really and personally? Do we know Jesus Christ as a person, and as a personal Savior? Do we know him by a heart acquaintance, and know him well? This, this only, is eternal life. And is Jesus glorified in us? Let us continue this personal inquiry. Do our lives prove his divinity? And does Jesus shine brighter because of us? Are we opaque or transparent bodies, and do we darken or reflect his pure light? Once more let us ask: Do we seek God's glory? Do we seek glory where Christ sought it? "Glorify thou me with thy own self." Do we esteem the presence and the possession of God our most excellent glory and our supreme good?

How closely does he bind himself and his Father to his people! His heart centers upon them in this high hour of holy communion with his Father.

> I have manifested thy name unto the men which thou gavest me out of the world; thine they were, and thou gavest them me; and they have kept thy word. Now they have known that

all things whatsoever thou hast given me are of thee. For I have given unto them the words which thou gavest me; and they have received them, and have known surely that I came out from thee, and they have believed that thou didst send me. I pray for them; I pray not for the world; but for them which thou hast given me; for they are thine. And all mine are thine, and thine are mine; and I am glorified in them (John 17:6–10).

He prays also for keeping for these disciples. Not only were they to be chosen, elected, and possessed, but were to be kept by the Father's watchful eyes and by the Father's omnipotent hand.

And now I am no more in the world, but these are in the world, and I come to thee. Holy Father, keep through thine own name those whom thou hast given me, that they may be one, as we are (John 17:11).

He prays that they might be kept by the holy Father, in all holiness by the power of his name. He asks that his people may be kept from sin, from all sin, from sin in the concrete and sin in the abstract, from sin in all its shapes of evil, from all sin in this world. He prays that they might not only be fit and ready for heaven, but ready and fit for earth, for its sweetest privileges, its sternest duties, its deepest sorrows, and its richest joys; ready for all of its trials, consolations, and triumphs. "I pray not that thou shouldest take them out of the world, but that thou shouldest keep them from the evil."

He prays that they may be kept from the world's greatest evil, which is sin. He desires that they may be kept from the guilt, the power, the pollution, and the punishment of sin. The Revised Version makes it read, "That thou shouldest keep them from the evil one." Kept from the devil, so that he might not touch them, nor find them, nor have a place in them; that they might be all owned, possessed, filled, and guarded by God. "Kept by the power of God through faith unto salvation."

He places us in the arms of his Father, on the bosom of his Father, and in the heart of his Father. He calls God into service, puts him to the front, and places us under his Father's closer keeping, under his Father's shadow, and under the covert of his Father's wing. The Father's rod and staff are for our security, for our comfort, for our refuge, for our strength and guidance.

These disciples were not to be taken out of the world, but kept from its evil, its monster evil, which is itself. "This present evil world." How the world seduces, dazzles, and deludes the children of men! His disciples are chosen out of the world, out of the world's bustle and earthliness, out of its all-devouring greed of gain, out of its money-desire, money-love, and money-toil. Earth draws and holds as if it was made out of gold and not out of dirt; as though it was covered with diamonds and not with graves.

"They are not of the world, even as I am not of the world." Not only from sin and Satan were they to be kept, but also from the soil, stain, and the taint of worldliness, as Christ was free from it. Their relation to Christ was not only to free them from the world's defiling taint, its unhallowed love, and its criminal friendships, but the world's hatred would inevitably follow their Christlikeness. No result so necessarily and universally follows its cause as this. "The world hath hated them because they are not of the world, even as I am not of the world."

How solemn and almost awful the repetition of the declaration, "They are not of the world, even as I am not of the world." How pronounced, radical, and eternal was our Lord Christ's divorce from the world! How pronounced, radical, and eternal is that of our Lord's true followers from the world! The world hates the disciple as it hated his Lord, and will crucify the disciple just as it crucified his Lord. How pertinent the question, Have we Christ's unworldliness? Does the world hate us as it hated our Lord? Are his words fulfilled in us?

If the world hate you, ye know that it hated me before it hated you. If ye were of the world, the world would love his own; but because ye are not of the world, but I have chosen you out of the world, therefore the world hateth you (John 15:18–19).

He puts himself before us clear-cut as the full portraiture of
an unworldly Christian. Here is our changeless pattern. "They
are not of the world even as I am not of the world." We must
be cut after this pattern.

The subject of their unity pressed on him. Note how he
called his Father's attention to it, and see how he pleaded for
this unity of his followers:

> And now I am no more in the world, but these are in the
> world and I come to thee. Holy Father, keep through thine
> own name those whom thou hast given me, that they may be
> one, as we are (John 17:11).

Again he returns to it as he sees the great crowds flocking to
his standard as the ages pass on:

> That they all may be one; as thou, Father, art in me, and I in
> thee, that they also may be one in us; that the world may
> believe that thou hast sent me. And the glory which thou
> gavest me I have given them; that they may be one, even as we
> are one. I in them and thou in me that they may be made per-
> fect in one; and that the world may know that thou hast sent
> me, and hast loved them, as thou hast loved me (John
> 17:21–23).

Notice how intently his heart was set on this unity. What
shameful history, and what bloody annals has this lack of unity
written for God's church! These walls of separations, these
alienations, these riven circles of God's family, these warring
tribes of men, and these internecine, fratricidal wars! He looks
ahead and sees how Christ is torn, how he bleeds and suffers
afresh in all these sad things of the future. The unity of God's
people was to be the heritage of God's glory promised to them.
Division and strife are the devil's bequest to the church, a heritage of failure, weakness, shame, and woe.

The oneness of God's people was to be the one credential to
the world of the divinity of Christ's mission on earth. Let us
ask in all candor, are we praying for this unity as Christ prayed
for it? Are we seeking the peace, the welfare, the glory, the

might, and the divinity of God's cause as it is found in the
unity of God's people?

Going back again, note, please, how he puts himself as the
exponent and the pattern of this unworldliness which he
prays may possess his disciples. He sends them into the world
just as his Father sent him into the world. He expects them to
be and do, just as he was and as he did for his Father. He
sought the sanctification of his disciples that they might be
wholly devoted to God and purified from all sin. He desired in
them a holy life and a holy work for God. He devoted himself
to death in order that they might be devoted in life to God.
For a true sanctification he prayed, a real, whole, and thorough sanctification, embracing soul, body, and mind, for time
and eternity. With him the word itself had much to do with
their true sanctification.

> Sanctify them through thy truth; thy word is truth. And for
> their sakes I sanctify myself, that they also might be sanctified
> by the truth (John 17:17, 19).

Entire devotedness was to be the type of their sanctification.
His prayer for their sanctification marks the pathway to full
sanctification. Prayer is that pathway. All the ascending steps
to that lofty position of entire sanctification are steps of prayer,
increasing prayerfulness in spirit and increasing prayerfulness
in fact. "Pray without ceasing is the imperative prelude to "the
very God of peace sanctify you wholly." And prayer is but the
continued interlude and doxology of this rich grace in the
heart:

> I pray God your whole spirit and soul and body be pre-
> served blameless unto the coming of our Lord Jesus Christ.
> Faithful is he that calleth you, who also will do it (1 Thess.
> 5:23–24).

We can only meet our full responsibilities and fulfill our
high mission when we go forth sanctified as Christ our Lord
was sanctified. He sends us into the world just as his Father
sent him into the world. He expects us to be as he was, to do

as he did, and to glorify the Father just as he glorified the Father.

What longings he had to have us with him in heaven: "Father, I will that they also whom thou hast given me, be with me where I am; that they may behold my glory, which thou hast given me." What response do our truant hearts make to this earnest, loving, Christly longing? Are we as eager for heaven as he is to have us there? How calm, how majestic, and how authoritative is his "I will"!

He closes his life with inimitable calmness, confidence, and sublimity. "I have glorified thee on the earth; I have finished the work which thou gavest me to do."

The annals of earth have nothing comparable to it in real serenity and sublimity. May we come to our end thus in supreme loyalty to Christ.

# 12

# The Gethsemane Prayer

WE now come to Gethsemane. What a contrast! The high-priestly prayer had been one of intense feelings of universal grasp, and of worldwide and illimitable sympathy and solicitude for his church. Perfect calmness and perfect poise reigned. Majestic he was and simple and free from passion or disquiet. The royal intercessor and advocate for others, his petitions are like princely edicts, judicial and authoritative. How changed now! In Gethsemane he seems to have entered another region, and becomes another man. His high-priestly prayer, so exquisite in its tranquil flow, so unruffled in its strong, deep current, is like the sun, moving in meridian, unsullied glory, brightening, vitalizing, ennobling, and blessing everything. The Gethsemane prayer is that same sun declining in the west, plunged into an ocean of storm and cloud, storm-covered, storm-eclipsed with gloom, darkness and terror on every side.

The prayer in Gethsemane is exceptional in every way. The super-incumbent load of the world's sin is upon him. The lowest point of his depression has been reached. The bitterest cup of all, his bitter cup, is being pressed to his lips. The weakness of all his weaknesses, the sorrow of all his sorrows, the agony of all his agonies are now upon him. The flesh is giving out with its fainting and trembling pulsations, like the trickling of his heart's blood. His enemies have thus far triumphed. Hell is in a jubilee and bad men are joining in the hellish carnival.

Gethsemane was Satan's hour, Satan's power, and Satan's darkness. It was the hour of massing all of Satan's forces for a final, last conflict. Jesus had said, "The prince of this world cometh and findeth nothing in me." The conflict for earth's mastery is before him. The spirit led and drove him into the stern conflict and severe temptation of the wilderness. But his comforter, his leader and his inspiration through his matchless history, seems to have left him now. "He began to be sorrowful and very heavy," and we hear him under this great pressure exclaiming, "My soul is exceeding sorrowful, even unto death." The depression, conflict, and agony had gone to the very core of his spirit, and had sunk him to the very verge of death. "Sore amazed" he was.

Surprise and awe depress his soul. "Very heavy" was the hour of hell's midnight which fell upon his spirit. Very heavy was this hour when all the sins of all the world, of every man, of all men, fell upon his immaculate soul, with all their stain and all their guilt.

He cannot abide the presence of his chosen friends. They cannot enter into the depths and demands of this fearful hour. His trusted and set watchers were asleep. His Father's face is hid. His Father's approving voice is silent. The Holy Spirit, who had been with him in all the trying hours of his life, seems to have withdrawn from the scene. Alone he must drink the cup, alone he must tread the winepress of God's fierce wrath and of Satan's power and darkness, and of man's envy, cruelty, and vindictiveness. The scene is well described by Luke:

> And he came out and went, as he was wont, to the Mount of Olives: and his disciples also followed him. And when he was at the place, he said unto them, Pray that ye enter not into temptation. And he was withdrawn from them about a stone's cast, and kneeled down and prayed, Saying, Father, if thou be willing remove this cup from me; nevertheless, not my will, but

thine, be done. And there appeared an angel unto him from heaven, strengthening him. And being in an agony he prayed more earnestly; and his sweat was as it were great drops of blood falling down to the ground. And when he rose up from prayer, and was come to his disciples, he found them sleeping for sorrow. And said unto them, Why sleep ye? Rise and pray, lest ye enter into temptation (Luke 22:39–46).

The prayer agony of Gethsemane crowns Calvary with glory. The prayers offered by Christ on the cross are the union of weakness and strength, of deepest agony and desolation, and are accompanied with sweetest calm, divinest submission, and implicit confidence.

Nowhere in prophet or priest, king or ruler, of synagogue or church, does the ministry of prayer assume such marvels of variety, power, and fragrance as in the life of Jesus Christ. It is the aroma of God's sweetest spices, aflame with God's glory, and consumed by God's will.

We find in this Gethsemane prayer that which we find nowhere else in the praying of Christ. "O my Father, if it be possible, let this cup pass from me; nevertheless, not as I will, but as thou wilt." This is different from the whole tenor and trend of his praying and doing. How different from his high-priestly prayer! "Father, I will," is the law and life of that prayer. In his last directions for prayer, he makes our will the measure and condition of prayer. If ye abide in me, and my words abide in you, ye shall ask what ye will, and it shall be done unto you." He said to the Syrophenician woman, "Great is thy faith! Be it unto thee as thou wilt."

But in Gethsemane his praying was against the declared will of God The pressure was so heavy upon him, the cup was so bitter, the burden was so strange and intolerable, that the flesh cried out for relief. Prostrate, sinking, sorrowful unto death. he sought to be relieved from that which seemed too heavy to bear. He prayed, however, not in revolt against God's will, but in submission to that will, and yet to change God's plan and to alter God's purposes he prayed. Pressed by the weakness of the flesh. and by the powers of hell in all their dire, hellish malignity, and might, Jesus was on this only one occasion constrained to pray against the will of God. He did it, though, with great wariness and pious caution. He did it with declared and inviolable submission to God's will. But this was exceptional.

Simple submission to God's will is not the highest attitude of the soul to God. Submission may be seeming, induced by conditions, nothing but an inforced surrender, not cheerful but grudging, only a temporary expedient, a fitful resolve. When the occasion or calamity which called it forth is removed, the will returns to its old ways and to its old self.

Jesus Christ prayed always with this one exception in conformity with the will of God. He was one with God's plan, and one with God's will. To pray in conformity with God's will was the life and law of Christ. The same was law of his praying. Conformity, to live one with God, is a far higher and diviner life than to live simply in submission to God. To pray in conformity—together with God—is a far higher and diviner way to pray than mere submission. At its best state, submission is non-rebellion, an acquiescence, which is good, but not the highest. The most powerful form of praying is positive, aggressive, mightily outgoing, and creative. It molds things, changes things, and brings things to pass.

Conformity means to "stand perfect and complete in all the will of God." It means to delight to do God's will, to run with eagerness and ardor to carry out his plans. Conformity to God's will involves submission, patient, loving, sweet submission. But submission in itself falls short of and does not include conformity. We may be submissive but not conformed. We may accept results against which we have warred, and even be resigned to them.

Conformity means to be one with God, both in result and in processes. Submission may be one with God in the end. Conformity is one with God in the beginning, and the end. Jesus had conformity, absolute and perfect, to God's will, and by that he prayed. This was the single point where there was a drawing back from God's processes, extorted by insupportable pain, fear, and weariness. His submission was abject, loyal, and confiding, as his conformity had been constant and perfect. Conformity is the only true submission, the most loyal, the sweetest, and the fullest.

Gethsemane has its lessons of humble supplications as Jesus knelt alone in the garden. Of burdened prostration, as he fell on his face, of intense agony, of distressing dread, of hesitancy and shrinking back, of crying out for relief—yet amid it all of cordial submission to God, accompanied with a singleness of purpose for his glory.

Satan will have for each of us his hour and power of darkness and for each of us the bitter cup and the fearful spirit of gloom.

We can pray against God's will, as Moses did, to enter the promised land; as Paul did about the thorn in the flesh; as David did for his doomed child; as Hezekiah did to live. We must pray against God's will when the stroke is the heaviest, the sorrow is the keenest, and the grief is the deepest. We may lie prostrate all night, as David did, through the hours of darkness. We may pray for hours, as Jesus did, and in the darkness of many nights, not measuring the hours by the clock, nor the nights by the calendar. It must all be, however, the prayer of submission.

When sorrow and the night and desolation of Gethsemane fall in heaviest gloom on us, we ought to submit patiently and tearfully, if need be, but sweetly and resignedly, without tremor, or doubt, to the cup pressed by a Father's hand to our lips. "Not my will, but thine, be done," our broken hearts shall say. In God's own way, mysterious to us, that cup has in its bitterest dregs, as it had for the Son of God, the gem and gold of perfection. We are to be put into the crucible to be refined. Christ was made perfect in Gethsemane, not by the prayer, but by the suffering. "For it became him to make the captain of their salvation perfect through suffering." The cup could not pass because the suffering must go on and yield its fruit of perfection. Through many an hour of darkness and of hell's power, through many a sore conflict with the prince of this world, by drinking many a bitter cup, we are to be made perfect. To cry out against the terrific and searching flame of the crucible of a Father's painful processes is natural and is no sin, if there be perfect acquiescence in the answer to our prayer, perfect submission to God's will, and perfect devotion to his glory.

If our hearts are true to God, we may plead with him about his way, and seek relief from his painful processes. But the fierce fire of the crucible and the agonizing victim with his agonizing and submissive prayer, is not the normal and highest form of majestic and all-commanding prayer. We can cry out in the crucible, and can cry out against the flame which purifies and perfects us. God allows this, hears this, and answers this, not by taking us out of the crucible, nor by mitigating the fierceness of the flame, but by sending more than an angel to strengthen us. And yet crying out thus, with full submission, does not answer the real high, worldwide, royal, and eternity-reaching behests of prayer.

The prayer of submission must not be so used as to vitiate or substitute the higher and mightier prayer of faith. Nor must it be so stressed as to break down importunate and prevailing prayer, which would be to disarm prayer of its efficiency and discrown its glorious results and would be to encourage listless, sentimental, and feeble praying.

We are ever ready to excuse our lack of earnest and toilsome praying by a fancied and delusive view of submission. We often end praying just where we ought to begin. We quit praying when God waits and is waiting for us to really pray. We are deterred by obstacles from praying, or we succumb to difficulties, and call it submission to God's will. A world of beggarly faith, of spiritual laziness, and of halfheartedness in prayer, is covered under the high and pious name of submission. To have no plan but to seek God's plan and carry it out, is of the essence and inspiration of Christlike praying. This is far more than putting in a clause of submission. Jesus did this once in seeking to change the purpose of God, but all his other praying was the output of being perfectly at one with the plans and purposes of God. It is after this order we pray when we abide in him and when his word abides in us. Then we ask what we will and it is done. It is then our prayers fashion and create things. Our wills then become God's will and his will becomes ours. The two become one, and there is not a note of discord.

"And this is the confidence that we have in him, that, if we ask anything according to his will, he heareth us." And if we know that he hears us, whatsoever we ask, we know that we have the petitions that we desired of him. And then it proves true: "And whatsoever we ask, we receive of him, because we keep his commandments, and do those things that are pleasing in his sight."

What restraint, forbearance, self-denial, and loyalty to duty to God, and what deference to the Old Testament Scriptures are in that statement of our Lord:

> Thinkest thou that I cannot now pray to my Father, and he shall presently give me more than twelve legions of angels? But how then shall the scriptures be fulfilled, that thus it must be? (Matt. 26:53–54).

# 13

# The Holy Spirit and Prayer

THE gospel without the Holy Spirit would be vain and negatory. The gift of the Holy Spirit was vital to the work of Jesus Christ in the atonement. As Jesus did not begin his work on earth till he was anointed by the Holy Spirit, so the same Holy Spirit is necessary to carry forward and make effective the atoning work of the Son of God. As his anointing by the Holy Spirit at his baptism was an era in his life, so also is the coming of the Holy Spirit at Pentecost a great era in the work of redemption in making effective the work of Christ's church.

The Holy Spirit is not only the bright lamp of the Christian dispensation, its teacher and guide, but it is also the divine helper.

He is the enabling agent in God's new dispensation of doing. As the pilot takes his stand at the wheel to guide the vessel, so the Holy Spirit takes up his abode in the heart to guide and empower all its efforts. The Holy Spirit executes the whole gospel through the man by his presence and control of the spirit of the man.

In the execution of the atoning work of Jesus Christ, in its general and more comprehensive operation, or in its minute and personal application, the Holy Spirit is the one efficient agent, absolute and indispensable.

The gospel cannot be executed but by the Holy Spirit. He only has the regal authority to do this royal work. Intellect cannot execute it; neither can learning, nor eloquence, nor truth, not even the revealed truth can execute the gospel. The marvelous facts of Christ's life told by hearts unanointed by the Holy Spirit will be dry and sterile, or "like a story told by an idiot, full of sound and fury, signifying nothing." Not even the precious blood can execute the gospel. Not any, nor all of these, though spoken with angelic wisdom, angelic eloquence, can execute the gospel with saving power. Only tongues set on fire by the Holy Spirit can witness the saving power of Christ with power to save others.

No one dared move from Jerusalem to proclaim or utter the message along its streets to the dying multitudes till the Holy Spirit came in baptismal power. John could not utter a word, though he had pillowed his head on Christ's bosom and caught the pulsations of Christ's heart, and though his brain was full of the wondrous facts of that life and of the wondrous words which fell from his lips. John must wait till a fuller and richer endowment than all of these came on him. Mary could not live over that Christ-life in the home of John, though she had nurtured the Christ and stored heart and mind full of holy and motherly memories, till she was empowered by the Holy Spirit.

The coming of the Holy Spirit is dependent upon prayer, for prayer can compass with its authority and demands only the realm where this person of the Godhead has his abode. Even Christ was subject to this law of prayer. With him, it is, it ever has been, and ever will be, "Ask, and it shall be given you; seek, and ye shall find; knock, and it shall be opened unto you." To his disconsolate disciples he said, "I will pray the Father, and he will give you another comforter." This law of prayer for the Holy Spirit presses on the master and on the disciples as well. Of so many of God's children it may truly be said, "Ye have him not because ye ask not." And of many others it might be said, "Ye have him in faint measure because ye pray for him in faint measure."

The Holy Spirit is the spirit of all grace and of each grace as well. Purity, power, holiness, faith, love, joy, and all grace are brought into being and perfected by him. Would we grow in grace in particular? Would we be perfect in all graces? We must seek the Holy Spirit by prayer.

We urge the seeking of the Holy Spirit. We need him, and we need to stir ourselves up to seek him. The measure we receive of him will be gauged by the fervor of faith and prayer with which we seek him. Our ability to work for God, and to pray to God, and live for God, and affect others for God will be dependent on the measure of the Holy Spirit received by us, dwelling in us, and working through us.

Christ lays down the clear and explicit law of prayer in this regard for all of God's children. The world needs the Holy Spirit to convict it of sin and of righteousness and judgment to come and to make it feel its guiltiness in God's sight. And this spirit of conviction on sinners comes in answer to the prayers of God's people. God's children need him more and more, need his life, his more abundant life, his super-abundant life. But that life begins and ever increases as the child of God prays for the Holy Spirit. "If ye, then, being evil, know how to give good gifts unto your children, how much more shall your heavenly Father give the Holy Spirit to them that ask him?" This is the law, a condition brightened by a promise and sweetened by a relationship.

The gift of the Holy Spirit is one of the benefits flowing to us from the glorious presence of Christ at the right hand of God, and this gift of the Holy Spirit, together with all the other gifts of the enthroned Christ, are secured to us by prayer as the condition. The Bible by express statement, as well as by its general principles and clear and constant intimations, teaches us that the gift of the Holy Spirit is connected with and conditioned in prayer. That the Holy Spirit is in the world as God is in the world, is true. That the Holy Spirit is in the world as Christ is in the world is also true. And it is also true that there is nothing predicated of him being in us and in the world that is not predicated of God and Christ being in us, and in the world. The Holy Spirit was in the world in measure before Pentecost, and in the measure of his operation then he was prayed for and sought for, and the principles are unchanged.

The truth is, if we cannot pray for the Holy Spirit we cannot pray for any good thing from God, for he is the sum of all good to us. The truth is we seek after the Holy Spirit just as we seek after God, just as we seek after Christ, with strong cryings and tears, and we are to seek always for more and more of his gifts, and power, and grace. The truth is that the presence and power of the Holy Spirit at any given meeting is conditioned on praying faith.

Christ lays down the doctrine that the reception of the Holy Spirit is conditioned on prayer, and he himself illustrated this universal law, for when the Holy Spirit came upon him at his baptism, he was praying. The apostolic church in action illustrates the same great truth.

A few days after Pentecost the disciples were in an agony of prayer, "and when they had prayed, the place was shaken where they were assembled together; and they were all filled with the Holy Spirit." This incident destroys every theory which denies prayer as the condition of the coming and re-coming of the Holy Spirit after Pentecost, and confirms the view that Pentecost as the result of a long struggle of prayer is illustrative and confirmatory that God's great and most precious gifts are conditioned on asking, seeking, knocking prayer—ardent, importunate prayer.

The same truth comes to the front very prominently in Philip's revival at Samaria. Though filled with joy by believing in Christ, and though received into the church by water baptism, they did not receive the Holy Spirit till Peter and John went down there and prayed with and for them.

Paul's praying was God's proof to Ananias that Paul was in a state which conditioned him to receive the Holy Spirit.

The Holy Spirit is not only our teacher, our inspirer, and our revealer in prayer, but the power of our praying in measure and force is measured by the Spirit's power working in us, as the will and work of God, according to God's good pleasure. In the third chapter of Ephesians, after the marvelous prayer of Paul for the church, he seemed to be apprehensive that they would think he had gone beyond the ability of God in his large asking. And so he closes his appeal for them with the words that God was "able to do exceeding abundantly above all that we ask or think." The power of God to do for us was measured by the power of God in us. "According to," says the apostle, that is, after the measure of, "the power that worketh in us." The projecting power of praying outwardly was the projecting power of God in us. The feeble operation of God in us brings feeble praying. The mightiest operation of God in us brings the mightiest praying. The secret of prayerlessness is the absence of the work of the Holy Spirit in us. The secret of feeble praying everywhere is the lack of God's Spirit in his mightiness.

The ability of God to answer and work through our prayers is measured by the divine energy that God has been enabled to put in us by the Holy Spirit. The projecting power of praying is the measure of the Holy Spirit in us. So the statement of James in the fifth chapter of his epistle is to this effect: "The fervent effectual prayer of a righteous man availeth much." The prayer wrought in the heart by the almighty energy of the Holy Spirit works mightily in its results just as Elijah's prayer did.

Would we pray efficiently and mightily? Then the Holy Spirit must work in us efficiently and mightily. Paul makes the principle of universal application. "Whereunto I also labor, striving according to his working, which worketh in me mightily." All labor for Christ which does not spring from the Holy Spirit working in us, is inconsequential and vain. Our prayers and activities are so feeble and resultless because he has not worked in us and cannot work in us his glorious work. Would you pray with mighty results? Seek the mighty workings of the Holy Spirit in your own spirit.

Here we have the initial lesson in prayer for the Holy Spirit which was to enlarge to its full fruitage in Pentecost. It is to be noted that in John 14:16, where Jesus engages to pray the Father to send another comforter, who would dwell with his disciples and be in them, that this is not a prayer that the Holy Spirit might do his work in making us children of God by regeneration, but it was for that fuller grace and power and person of the Holy Spirit which we can claim by virtue of our relation as children of God. His work in us to make us the children of God and his person abiding with us and in us, as children of God, are entirely different stages of the same Spirit in his relation to us. In this latter work, his gifts and works are greater, and his presence, even himself, is greater than his works or gifts. His work in us prepares us for himself. His gifts are the dispensations of his presence. He puts and makes us members of the body of Christ by his work. He keeps us in that body by his presence and person. He enables us to discharge the functions as members of that body by his gifts.

The whole lesson culminates in asking for the Holy Spirit as the great objective point of all praying. In the direction in the Sermon on the Mount, we have the very plain and definite promise, "If ye, being evil, know how to give good gifts unto your children, how much more shall your Father in heaven give good things to them that ask him?" In Luke we have "good things" substituted by "the Holy Spirit." All good is comprehended in the Holy Spirit and he is the sum and climax of all good things.

How complex, confusing, and involved is many a human direction about obtaining the gift of the Holy Spirit as the abiding comforter, our sanctifier and the one who empowers us. How simple and direct is our Lord's direction—ASK! This is plain and direct. Ask with urgency, ask without fainting. Ask, seek, knock, till he comes. Your heavenly Father will surely send him if you ask for him. Wait in the Lord for the Holy Spirit. It is the child waiting, asking, urging, and praying perseveringly for the Father's greatest gift and for the child's greatest need, the Holy Spirit.

How are we to obtain the Holy Spirit so freely promised to those who seek him believingly? Wait, press, and persevere with all the calmness and with all the ardor of a faith which knows no fear, which allows no doubt, a faith which staggers not at the promise through unbelief, a faith which in its darkest and most depressed hours against hope believes in hope, which is brightened by hope and strengthened by hope, and which is saved by hope.

Wait and pray—here is the key which unlocks every castle of despair, and which opens every treasure store of God. It is the simplicity of the child's asking of the Father, who gives with a largeness, liberality, and cheerfulness, infinitely above everything ever known to earthly parents. Ask for the Holy Spirit—seek for the Holy Spirit—knock for the Holy Spirit. He is the Father's greatest gift for the child's greatest need.

In these three words, *ask, seek,* and *knock,* given us by Christ, we have the repetition of the advancing steps of insistency and effort. He is laying himself out in command and promise in the strongest way, showing us that if we will lay ourselves out in prayer and will persevere, rising to higher and stronger attitudes and sinking to deeper depths of intensity and effort, that the answer must inevitably come. So that it is true the stars would fail to shine before the asking, the seeking, and the knocking would fail to obtain what is needed and desired.

There is no elect company here, only the election of undismayed, importunate, never-fainting effort in prayer: "For to him that knocketh, it shall be opened." Nothing can be stronger than this declaration assuring us of the answer unless it be the promise upon which it is based, "And I say unto you, ask and it shall be given you."

# 14

# The Holy Spirit, Our Helper in Prayer

ONE of the revelations of the New Testament concerning the Holy Spirit is that he is our helper in prayer. So we have in the following incident in our Lord's life the close connection between the Holy Spirit's work and prayer :

> In that hour Jesus rejoiced in spirit, and said, I thank thee, O Father, Lord of heaven and earth, that thou hast hid these things from the wise and prudent, and hast revealed them unto babes; even so, Father, for so it seemed good in thy sight (Luke 10:21).

Here we have revelations of what God is to us. Only the child's heart can know the Father, and only the child's heart can reveal the Father. It is by prayer only that all things are delivered to us by the Father through the Son. It is only by prayer that all things are revealed to us by the Father and by the Son. It is only in prayer that the Father gives himself to us, which is much more every way than all other things whatsoever.

The Revised Version reads: "At that same hour Jesus rejoiced in the Holy Spirit." This sets forth that great truth not generally known, or if known, ignored, that Jesus Christ was generally led by the Holy Spirit, and that his joy and his praying, as well as his working, and his life, were under the inspiration, law, and guidance of the Holy Spirit.

Turn to and read Romans 8:2b:

> Likewise the spirit also helpeth our infirmities; for we know not what we should pray for as we ought.

This text is most pregnant and vital, and needs to be quoted. Patience, hope, and waiting help us in prayer. But the greatest and the divinest of all helpers is the Holy Spirit. He takes hold of things for us. We are dark and confused, ignorant and weak in many things, in fact in everything pertaining to the heavenly life, especially in the simple service of prayer. There is an "ought" on us, an obligation, a necessity to pray, a spiritual necessity upon us of the most absolute and imperative kind. But we do not feel the obligation and have no ability to meet it. The Holy Spirit helps us in our weaknesses, gives wisdom to our ignorance, turns ignorance into wisdom, and changes our weakness into strength. The Spirit himself does this. He helps and takes hold with us as we tug and toil. He adds his wisdom to our ignorance, gives his strength to our weakness. He pleads for us and in us. He quickens, illumines, and inspires our prayers. He proclaims and elevates the matter of our prayers, and inspires the words and feelings of our prayers. He works mightily in us so that we can pray mightily. He enables us to pray always and ever according to the will of God.

In 1 John 5:14–15 we have these words:

> And this is the confidence that we have in him, that, if we ask any thing according to his will, he heareth us: And if we know that he hear us, whatsoever we ask, we know that we have the petitions that we desired of him.

That which gives us boldness and so much freedom and fullness of approach toward God, the fact and basis of that boldness and liberty of approach, is that we are asking "according to the will of God." This does not mean submission, but conformity. "According to" means after the standard, conformity, agreement. We have boldness and all freedom of access to God because we are praying in conformity to his will. God records his general will in his Word, but he has this special work in praying for us to do. His "things are prepared for us," as the prophet says, who "wait upon him." How can we know the will of God in our praying? What are the things which God designs specially for us to do and pray? The Holy Spirit reveals them to us perpetually.

> The Spirit itself maketh intercession for us with groanings which cannot be uttered. And he that searcheth the hearts knoweth what is the mind of the Spirit, because he maketh intercession for the saints according to the will of God (Rom. 8:26–27).

Combine this text with those words of Paul in 1 Corinthians 2:9–16:

> But as it is written, Eye hath not seen, nor ear heard, neither have entered into the heart of man, the things which God hath prepared for them that love him. But God hath revealed them unto us by his Spirit; for the Spirit searcheth all things, yea, the deep things of God. For what man knoweth the things of a man, save the spirit of man which is in him? Even so the things of God knoweth no man, but the Spirit of God. Now we have received, not the spirit of the world, but the spirit which is of God; that we might know the things that are freely given to us of God. Which things also we speak, not in the words which man's wisdom teacheth, but which the Holy Ghost teacheth, comparing spiritual things with spiritual. But the natural man receiveth not the things of the Spirit of God; for they are foolishness unto him; neither can he know them, because they are spiritually discerned. But he that is spiritual judgeth all things, yet he himself is judged of no man. For who hath known the mind of the Lord, that he may instruct him? But we have the mind of Christ.

"Revealed to us by the Spirit." Note those words. God searches the heart where the Spirit dwells and knows the mind of the Spirit. The Spirit who dwells in our hearts searches the deep purposes and the will of God, and reveals those purposes and will of God to us, that we might know the things which are freely given to us of God. Our spirits are so fully indwelt by the Spirit of God, so responsive and obedient to his illumination and to his will, that we ask with holy boldness and freedom the things which the Spirit of God has shown us as the will of God, and faith is assured. Then we know that "we have the petitions that we have asked."

The natural man prays, but prays according to his own will, fancy, and desire. If he has ardent desires and groanings, they are the fire and agony of nature simply, and not that of the Spirit. What a world of natural praying there is, which is selfish, self-centered, self-inspired! The Spirit, when he prays through us, or helps us to meet the mighty "oughtness" of right praying, trims our praying down to the will of God, and then we give heart and expression to his unutterable groanings. Then we have the mind of Christ, and pray as he would pray. His thoughts, purposes, and desires are our desires, purposes, and thoughts.

This is not a new and different Bible from that which we already have, but it is the Bible we have, applied personally by the Spirit of God. It is not new texts, but rather the Spirit's embellishing of certain texts for us at the time.

It is the unfolding of the word by the Spirit's light, guidance, teaching, enabling us to perform the great office of intercessors on earth, in harmony with the great intercessions of Jesus Christ at the Father's right hand in heaven.

We have in the Holy Spirit an illustration and an enabler of what this intercession is and ought to be. We are charged to supplicate in the Spirit and to pray in the Holy Spirit. We are reminded that the Holy Spirit "helpeth our infirmities," and that while intercession is an art of so divine and so high a nature that though we know not what to pray for as we ought, yet the Spirit teaches us this heavenly science by making intercession in us "with groanings which cannot be uttered." How burdened these intercessions of the Holy Spirit! How profoundly he feels the world's sin, the world's woe, and the world's loss, and how deeply he sympathizes with the dire conditions, are seen in his groanings which are too deep for utterance and too sacred to be voiced by him. He inspires us to this most divine work of intercession, and his strength enables us to sigh unto God for the oppressed, the burdened, and the distressed creation. The Holy Spirit helps us in many ways.

How intense will be the intercessions of the saints who supplicate in the spirit! How vain and delusive and how utterly fruitless and inefficient are prayers without the Spirit! Official prayers they may be, fitted for state occasions, beautiful and courtly, but worth less than nothing as God values prayer.

It is our unfainting praying which will help the Holy Spirit to his mightiest work in us, and at the same time he helps us to these strenuous and exalted efforts in prayer.

We can and do pray by many inspirations and in many ways which are not of God. Many prayers are stereotyped in manner and in matter, in part, if not as a whole. Many prayers are hearty and vehement, but it is natural heartiness and a fleshly vehemence. Much praying is done by dint of habit and through form. Habit is a second nature and holds to the good, when so directed, as well as to the bad. The habit of praying is a good habit, and should be early and strongly formed; but to pray by habit merely is to destroy the life of prayer and allow it to degenerate into a hollow and sham-producing form. Habit may form the bank for the river of prayer, but there must be a strong, deep, pure current, crystal and life-giving, flowing between these two banks. Hannah multiplied her praying, "but she poured out her soul before the Lord." We cannot make our prayer habits too marked and controlling if the life-waters be full and overflow the banks.

Our divine example in praying is the Son of God. Our divine helper in praying is the Holy Spirit. He quickens us to pray and helps us in praying. Acceptable prayer must be begun and carried on by his presence and inspiration. We are enjoined in the Holy Scriptures to "pray in the Holy Spirit." We are charged to "pray always with all prayer and supplication in the Spirit." We are reminded for our encouragement, that "Likewise the Spirit also helpeth our infirmities: for we know not what we should pray for as we ought: but the Spirit itself maketh intercession for us with groanings which cannot be uttered. And he that searcheth the hearts knoweth what is the mind of the Spirit, because he maketh intercession for the saints according to the will of God."

So ignorant are we in this matter of prayer; so impotent are all other teachers to impart its lessons to our understanding and heart, that the Holy Spirit comes as the infallible and all-wise teacher to instruct us in this divine art. To pray with all your heart and all your strength, with the reason and the will, this is the greatest achievement of the Christian warfare on earth. This is what we are taught to do and enabled to do by the Holy Spirit. If no man can say that Jesus is the Christ but by the Spirit's help; for the much greater reason can no man pray save by the aid of God's Spirit. My mother's lips, now sealed by death, taught me many sweet lessons of prayer; prayers which have bound and held our hearts like golden threads; but these prayers, flowing through the natural chan-nel of a mother's love, cannot serve the purposes of my man-hood's warring, stormy life. These maternal lessons are but the ABCs of praying. For the higher and graduating lessons in prayer we must have the Holy Spirit. He only can unfold to us the mysteries of the prayer life, its duty and its service.

To pray by the Holy Spirit we must have him always. He does not, like earthly teachers, teach us the lesson and then withdraw. He stays to help us practice the lesson he has taught. We pray, not by the precepts and lessons he has taught, but we pray by him. He is both teacher and lesson. We can only know the lesson because he is ever with us to inspire, to illumine, to explain, to help us to do. We pray not by the truth the Holy Spirit reveals to us, but we pray by the actual presence of the Holy Spirit. He puts the desire in our hearts; kindles that desire by his own flame. We simply give lip and voice and heart to his unutterable groanings. Our prayers are taken up by him and energized and sanctified by his intercession. He prays for us, through us, and in us. We pray by him, through him, and in him. He puts the prayer in us and we give it utterance and heart.

We always pray according to the will of God when the Holy Spirit helps our praying. He prays through us only "according to the will of God." If our prayers are not according to the will of God they die in the presence of the Holy Spirit. He gives such prayers no countenance, no help. Discountenanced and unhelped by him, prayers, not according to God's will, soon die out of every heart where the Holy Spirit dwells.

We must, as Jude says, "Pray in the Holy Spirit." As Paul says, "with all prayer and supplication in the Spirit." Never forgetting that "the Spirit also helpeth our infirmities; for we know not what we should pray for as we ought: but the Spirit itself maketh intercession for us with groanings which cannot be uttered." Above all, over all, and through all our praying there must be the name of Christ, which includes the power of his blood, the energy of his intercession, the fullness of the enthroned Christ. "Whatsoever ye ask in my name that will I do."

# 15

## The Two Comforters and Two Advocates

THE fact that man has two divine comforters, advocates, helpers, is declarative of the affluence of God's provisions in the gospel, and also declarative of the settled purpose of God to execute his work of salvation with efficacy and final success. Many-sided are the infirmities and needs of man in his pilgrimage and warfare for heaven. These two Christs can meet with manifold wisdom.

The affluence of God's provision of two intercessors in executing the plan of salvation finds its counterpart in the prayer promise in its unlimited nature, comprehending all things, great and small.

"All things whatsoever ye ask in prayer, believing, ye shall receive." All things we have in Christ, all things we have in the Holy Spirit, and all things we have in prayer.

How much is ours in God's plan and purposes we have in these two Christs, the one ascended to heaven and enthroned, there to intercede for our benefit, the other Christ, his representative, and better substitute, on earth, to work in us and make intercessions for us!

The first Christ was a person. The other Christ, a person, but not clothed in physical form nor subject to human limitations as the first Christ necessarily was. Transient and local was the first

Christ. The other Christ not limited to locality, not transient, but abiding; not dealing with the sensible, the material, the fleshly, but entering personally into the mysterious and imperial domain of the spirit, to emancipate and transform into more than Eden beauty that waste and dark realm. The first Christ left his novitiates that they might enter into higher regions of spiritual knowledge. The man Christ withdrew that the spirit Christ might train and school into the deeper mysteries of God; that all the historical and physical might be transmuted into the pure gold of the spiritual. The first Christ brought to us a picture of what we must be. The other Christ mirrored this perfect and fadeless image on our hearts. The first Christ, like David, gathered and furnished the material for the temple. The other Christ out of this material forms God's glorious temple.

The possibilities of prayer, then, are the possibilities of these two divine intercessors. Where are the limitations to results when the Holy Spirit intercedes for us with groanings which cannot be uttered, when he so helps us that our prayers run parallel to the will of God, and we pray for the very things and in the very manner in which we ought to pray, schooled in and pressed to these prayers by the urgency of the Holy Spirit! How measureless are the possibilities of prayer when we are filled with all the fullness of God; when we stand perfect and complete in all the will of God?

If the intercession of Moses so wondrously preserved the being and safety of Israel throughout its marvelous history and destiny, what may we not secure through our intercessor, who is so much greater than Moses? All that God has lies open to Christ through prayer. All that Christ has lies open to us through prayer.

If we have the two Christs covering the whole realm of goodness, power, purity, and glory, in heaven and on earth—if we have the better Christ with us here in this world—why is it that we sigh to know the Christ after the flesh as the disciples knew him? Why is it that the mighty work of these two almighty intercessors finds us so barren of heavenly fruit, so feeble in all Christlike principles, so low in the Christlike life, and so marred in the Christlike image? Is it not because our prayers for the Holy Spirit have been so faint and few? The heavenly Christ can come to us in full beauty and power only when we have received the fullness of the present earthly Christ, even the Holy Spirit.

Living always the life of prayer, breathing always the spirit of prayer, being always in the fact of prayer, praying always in the Holy Spirit, the heavenly Christ would become ours by a clearer vision, a deeper love, and a more intimate fellowship than he was to his disciples in the days of his flesh.

We would not disguise nor abate the fact that there is a loss to us by our absent Christ as we will see and know him in heaven. But in our earthly work to be done by us, and above all to be done in us, we will know Christ and the Father better, and can better utilize them by the ministry of the Holy Spirit than would have been possible under the personal, human presence of the Son. So to the loving and obedient ones who are filled with the Spirit, both the Father and the Son "will come unto us and make their abode with us." In the day of the fullness of the indwelling Spirit, "Ye shall know that I am in my Father and ye in me and I in you." Amazing oneness and harmony, wrought by the almighty power of the other Christ!

There is not a note in the archangel's song to which the Holy Spirit does not attune man into sympathy, not a pulsation in the heart of God to which the Holy Spirit-filled heart does not respond with loud amens and joyful hallelujahs. Even more than this, by the other Christ, the Holy Spirit, "we know the love of Christ which passeth knowledge." More than this, by the Holy Spirit we are "filled with all the fullness of God." More than this, God is able to do exceeding abundantly above all that we ask or think according to the power of the Holy Spirit which worketh in us.

The presence and power of the other Christ would more than compensate the disciples for the loss of the first Christ. His going away had filled their hearts with a strange sorrow. A loneliness and desolation like an orphan's woe had swept over their hearts and stunned and bewildered them; but he comforted them by telling them that the Holy Spirit would be like the pains of a travailing mother, all forgotten in the untold joy that a manchild was born into the world.

# 16

# Prayer and
# the Holy Spirit Dispensation

THE dispensation of the Holy Spirit was ushered in by prayer. Read these words from Acts 1:13—"And when they were come in, they went up into an upper room, where abode both Peter, and James, and John, and Andrew, Philip, and Thomas, Bartholomew, and Matthew, James, the son of Alphaeus, and Simon Zelotes, and Judas the brother of James. These all continued with one accord in prayer and supplication, with the women, and Mary the mother of Jesus, and with his brethren."

This was the attitude which the disciples assumed after Jesus had ascended to heaven. That meeting for prayer ushered in the dispensation of the Holy Spirit, to which prophets had looked forward with entranced vision. And to prayer in a marked way has this dispensation, which holds in its keeping the fortune of the gospel, been committed.

Apostolic men knew well the worth of prayer and were jealous of the most sacred offices which infringed on their time and strength and hindered them from "giving themselves continually to prayer and to the ministry of the Word." They put prayer first. The Word depends on prayer that it "may have free course and be glorified." Praying apostles make preaching apostles. Prayer gives edge, entrance, and weight to the Word.

Sermons conceived by prayer and saturated with prayer are weighty sermons. Sermons may be ponderous with thought, sparkle with the gems of genius and of taste, pleasing and popular, but unless they have their birth and life in prayer, for God's uses, they are trifles, dull and dead.

The Lord of the harvest sends out laborers, full in number and perfect in kind, in answer to prayer. It needs no prophetic ken to declare that if the church had used prayer force to its utmost the light of the gospel would have long since girdled the world.

God's gospel has always waited more on prayer than on anything else for its successes. A praying church is strong though poor in all besides. A prayerless church is weak though rich in all besides. Only praying hearts will build God's kingdom. Only praying hands will put the crown on the Savior's head.

The Holy Spirit is the divinely appointed substitute for and representative of the personal and humanized Christ. How much is he to us! And how we are to be filled by him, live in him, walk in him, and be led by him! How we are to conserve and kindle to a brighter and more consuming glow the holy flame! How careful should we be never to quench that pure flame! How watchful, tender, loving ought we to be so as not to grieve his sensitive, loving nature! How attentive, meek, and obedient, never to resist his divine impulses, always to hear his voice, and always to do his divine will. How can all this be done without much and continuous prayer?

The importunate widow had a great case to win against helpless, hopeless despair, but she did it by importunate prayer. We have this great treasure to preserve and enhance, but we have a divine person to entertain and help. We can be enabled to meet our duties only by much prayer.

Prayer is the only element in which the Holy Spirit can live and work. Prayer is the golden chain which happily enslaves him to his happy work in us.

Everything depends upon our having this second Christ, and retaining him in the fullness of his power. With the disciples, Pentecost was made by prayer. With them, Pentecost was continued by giving themselves to continued prayer. Persistent and unwearied prayer is the price we will have to pay for our Pentecost, by instant and continued prayer. Abiding in the fact and in the spirit of prayer is the only surety of our abiding in pentecostal power and purity.

Not only should the many-sided operation of the Holy Spirit in us and for us teach us the necessity of prayer for him, but also his condition with our praying assumes another attitude, the attitude of mutual dependence, that of action and reaction. The more we pray the more he helps us to pray, and the larger the measure of himself he gives to us. We are not only to pray and press and wait for his coming to us, but after we have received him in his fullness, we are to pray for a fuller and still larger bestowment of himself to us. We are to pray for the largest and ever-increasing and constant fullness of capacity. "That ye might be strengthened with might by his Spirit in the inner man," as Paul prayed for the Spirit-baptized Ephesian church. It will be remembered that he also prayed that Christ might dwell in your hearts by faith, rooted and grounded in love, measuring up to the breadth, length, depth, and height of the most perfect sainthood, and up to the immeasurable love of Christ, being filled with all the fullness of God.

In that wonderful prayer for those Christians, Paul laid himself out to pray to God, and by prayer he sought to fathom the fathomless depths and to measure the illimitable purposes and benefits of God's plan of salvation for immortal souls by the presence and work of the Holy Spirit. Only importunate and invincible prayer can bring the Holy Spirit to us, and secure for us these ineffably gracious results. "Epaphras always laboring fervently in prayers, that ye may stand perfect and complete in all the will of God."

The Word of God provides for a mighty, consciously realized religion in his saints, into whose happy, shining spirits God has been brought as a dweller, and whose heaven-toned lives have been attuned to melody by God's own hand.

Then will it prove true: "He that believeth on me, out of his belly shall flow rivers of living water." Here is a promise concerning the indwelling and outflowing of the Holy Spirit in us,

life-giving, fruitful, irresistible, a ceaseless outflow of the river
of God in us.

How God needs, how the world needs, how the church
needs the flow of this mighty river, more blessed than the Nile,
deeper, broader, more overflowing than the Amazon's broad and
mighty current! And yet what mere rills we are and have!

Oh, that the church by the infilling and outflowing of the
Holy Spirit might be able to raise up everywhere memorials of
the Holy Spirit's power, which might fix the eye as well as
engage the heart! We need, the age needs, the church needs,
memorials of God's mighty power, which will silence the enemy
and the avenger, dumbfound God's foes, strengthen weak
saints, and fill strong ones with triumphant raptures.

A glance at some more of the divine promises concerning
this vital question would show us how they need to be pro-
jected into the experimental and the actual. "If any man will do
his will, he shall know of the doctrine, whether it be of God or
whether I speak of myself." How we do need a conscious religion, personal and vital, unspeakable in its joy, and full of
glory! The need is for a conscious religion, made so by the
Spirit bearing witness that we are the children of God. A religion of "I know" is the only powerful, vital, and aggressive religion. "One thing I know, whereas I once was blind, but now I
see." We need men and women in these loose days who can
verify the above mentioned promise of Christ in their inner
consciousness. And yet how many untold thousands of people
in all of our churches, who have only a dim, impalpable, hope
so, maybe so, I trust so, kind of religion, all dubious, intangible,
and unstable.

There is certainly a great need in these days in the modern
church, first, for Christians to see and seek and obtain the high
privilege in the gospel of a heaven-born, clear-cut, and happy
religious experience, born of the presence of the Holy Spirit,
giving an undoubted assurance of sins forgiven, and of adop-
tion into the family of God.

And secondly, there is a need, subsequent to this conscious
realization of divine favor in the forgiveness of sins, and added
to it, of the reception of the Holy Spirit in his fullness, purifying

their hearts by faith, perfecting them in love, overcoming the world, and bestowing a divine, inward power over all sin, both inward and outward, and giving boldness to bear witness and qualifying for real religious service in the church and in the world.

There is a fearfully prevailing agnosticism in the church at this time. We greatly fear that a vast majority of our church members are now in this school of spiritual agnosticism, and really deem it to be a virtue to be there. God's Word gives no encouragement whatever to a shadowy religion and a vague religious experience. It calls us definitely into the realm of knowledge. It crowns religion with the crown of "I know." It passes us from the darkness of sin, doubt, and inward misgiving into the marvelous light, where we see clearly and know fully our personal relations to God.

> The things unknown to feeble sense,
> Unseen by reason's glimmering ray,
> With strong, commanding confidence,
> Their heavenly origin display.

Two things may be said just here in concluding this part of our study on this subject: First, this sort of biblical religion, heretofore described, comes directly through the office of the Holy Spirit dealing personally with each soul; and secondly, the Holy Spirit in all of his offices pertaining to spiritual life and religious experience is secured by earnest, definite, prevailing prayer.